# The College Instructor's Guide to Writing Test Items

*The College Instructor's Guide to Writing Test Items: Measuring Student Learning* addresses the need for direct and clear guidance on item writing for assessing broad ranges of content in many fields. By focusing on multiple-choice items, this book provides college instructors the tools to understand, develop, and use assessment activities in classrooms in a way that consistently supports learning. Including dozens of example items and additional resources to support the item-development process, this volume is unique in its practical-focus and is essential reading for instructors and soon-to-be educators, professional development specialists, and higher education researchers. As teaching, assessment, and learning are inherently intertwined, *The College Instructor's Guide to Writing Test Items* both facilitates the development of instructors' own practice and improves the learning outcomes and success of students.

**Michael C. Rodriguez** is the Campbell Leadership Chair in Education and Human Development and Professor of Educational Psychology at the University of Minnesota, USA.

**Anthony D. Albano** is Assistant Professor of Educational Psychology in the College of Education and Human Sciences at the University of Nebraska-Lincoln, USA.

# The College Instructor's Guide to Writing Test Items

## Measuring Student Learning

Michael C. Rodriguez and
Anthony D. Albano

Routledge
Taylor & Francis Group

NEW YORK AND LONDON

First published 2017
by Routledge
711 Third Avenue, New York, NY 10017

and by Routledge
2 Park Square, Milton Park, Abingdon, Oxon, OX14 4RN

*Routledge is an imprint of the Taylor & Francis Group, an informa business*

© 2017 Taylor & Francis

*Library of Congress Cataloging-in-Publication Data*
A catalog record for this book has been requested

ISBN: 978-1-138-88652-0 (hbk)
ISBN: 978-1-138-88653-7 (pbk)
ISBN: 978-1-315-71477-6 (ebk)

Typeset in Goudy
by Apex CoVantage, LLC

MIX
Paper from
responsible sources
FSC     FSC™ C013985
www.fsc.org

Printed in the United Kingdom
by Henry Ling Limited

# Contents

# Preface

College instructors, and institutions of higher education in general, are required to assess student learning outcomes for a number of purposes, including everything from grading to reporting to accreditation agencies. But most of us simply want to make sure students are getting it—or that our instructional practices are making a difference and helping students understand the subject matter—to achieve the learning outcomes intended by the course.

There are a number of books available regarding assessment in higher education. These mostly constitute efforts to contribute to systems-level assessments, as institutions of higher education are required to assess student learning outcomes by accreditation agencies and, in some cases, state legislatures. Some of these texts also contain information and guidance for classroom instructors, but these tend to be embedded in much larger volumes, still with the focus on institutional reporting. Even so, most authors have avoided providing many examples, and no book exists with research-based guidance and examples from multiple fields.

We hope to address the need for direct and clear guidance on item writing by focusing on multiple-choice response items, as they provide the fastest methods of assessing broad ranges of content in many fields. Minute for minute of testing, we get the most information about what students know and can do through carefully constructed multiple-choice items. To support this effort, we provide dozens of example items, some of them flawed, along with their improved counterparts. We also provide additional resources online at proola.org. Proola is a web application that supports instructors in the item development process, with resources for practicing and getting feedback while writing items.

We hope to reach everyone that creates, uses, and interprets assessments in higher education settings.

## College Instructors

The intended audience is broadly defined as college instructors. This includes faculty, lecturers, and anyone in an instructor position at an institution of higher education such as a community college, liberal arts college, or comprehensive university, including instructors of undergraduate- and graduate-level courses.

## Future Faculty Training Programs

Most comprehensive universities have programs that prepare graduate students for faculty positions. Programs like these are commonly facilitated by centers for teaching and learning. This text provides a deep treatment of classroom test development with examples from a wide range of fields.

## Centers for Teaching and Learning

Many colleges and universities have centers for teaching and learning that provide workshops, training opportunities, and resources to support the teaching and learning activities across campus. Many of these centers also provide guidance on classroom assessment, and we have reviewed this guidance from dozens of institutions hosting such resources. This text should serve as a more comprehensive resource to support the development of training programs for college instructors.

## Higher Education Researchers

Another important audience includes researchers in the areas of teaching and learning in higher education. The current attention to assessment of learning outcomes has inspired new research on the role of assessment in the higher education classroom. Researchers will find evidence-based guidance on principles of higher education assessment and principles of test item writing (to the extent that such research evidence exists). This will support those researchers creating or using classroom tests in their research and, of course, those conducting research directly on classroom assessment in higher education (if this might be you, please contact us and tell us about your work).

## Graduate Students

Finally, another potential audience includes graduate students interested in developing skills as future faculty or future college instructors at any level. Often graduate students are given opportunities to instruct undergraduate courses (and sometimes introductory graduate courses). But they are rarely prepared for the many tasks instructors must tackle, including item writing and test development.

# Acknowledgments

We must acknowledge and thank Tom Haladyna, our colleague and mentor. Tom was gracious enough to include us in an item-writing workshop for the National Council on Measurement in Education and in a number of publication opportunities. His extensive experience from research and practice in item writing provide a significant portion of evidence for the guidance presented in this book.

We also acknowledge the many colleagues and students who have contributed to our own understanding of the role of item writing in the college classroom and effective item-writing practices. Some of them have contributed example items throughout this book.

We thank the many contributors to Proola, the online item-development and -sharing tool that will be introduced and accessed throughout the book. Proola provides a way for instructors at all levels to share, edit, and obtain test items in numerous content areas. It promises to provide an important vehicle for a learning community focused on the practice of high-quality item writing. You can access Proola at http://proola.org.

# Introduction

Assessment has always been an important part of learning. In primary and secondary education, teachers use quizzes, tests, and many other forms of assessment for a variety of purposes, including supporting grading, informing instruction, and ultimately improving learning. In the research on classroom assessment, we know that coherent and integrated routines of instruction and assessment can maximize learning. However, few primary and secondary teachers are prepared to understand, develop, and use assessment activities in classrooms in a way that consistently supports learning. At the college level, instructors are even less prepared.

Nationally, we are in the midst of a debate regarding learning outcomes in higher education and, most importantly, how to assess and provide evidence of learning outcomes. Policy makers and the public in general have raised questions of whether students are actually learning or benefitting from their college educations, particularly given the rising costs of higher education. Although learning outcomes may vary in their labels and definitions across institutions, they commonly require that students gain content knowledge or *subject-matter expertise*. This outcome, more than most others, is a clear product of successful instruction and course-based learning.

College instructors now have at their disposal many options for administering test questions. This can occur in the midst of a lecture or class activity through the use of "clickers" or other classroom response systems, including handheld devices such as smartphones, tablets, or laptop computers. In a typical class, test questions are more frequently administered through quizzes and exams, including notorious final exams that can make or break a grade. And the quizzes and tests of today can be administered online through any number of internet-based course-support tools or learning-management systems (Blackboard, Canvas, Desire2Learn, Moodle, etc.). With the growing availability of online courses, online degrees, and online universities, the use of selected-response item formats is increasingly a core component of assessment.

The test question format of choice for many of these instructional technology and online systems is the multiple-choice (MC) item, in large part due to the ease of administration and scoring. However, as we have learned from experimental studies of item writing, the construction of the MC item is not necessarily as easy as it may appear. We have all experienced college test questions that leave us wondering if we are in the right class!

We strive to speak plainly and directly to college instructors to provide practical and high-quality guidance on writing test questions. To achieve the promise of high-quality teaching and learning, this guidance must be technically accurate and evidence based, as well as consistent with professional standards of educational measurement and student assessment. This is our goal.

This book contains many example test questions including poorly written items with edited and improved versions—for instructional purposes. But we hope you find that the bulk of the example test questions demonstrate the application of item-writing guidelines and that these are useful guides for your own courses.

## Assessment vs. Testing

We make a simple distinction between the broad concept of assessment and the much narrower concept of testing. A test is a collection of questions or tasks (which we generically call items), targeted to measure (provide quantifiable information about) learning objectives or some other trait. In our context of college classrooms, this typically includes knowledge, skills, and abilities, and maybe dispositions. Assessment is a broader concept, including quantitative and qualitative methods of collecting information formally or informally about any range of human cognitive or affective traits. For example, assessment could be performance based, where students engage in complex experiments, give multimedia presentations, or construct a portfolio of work over time; and assessment can also be done by watching students and listening to group discussions, interviewing students, or having students do a self-assessment of their achievement of course learning objectives. A test is one method of conducting assessment.

Our focus here is on college classroom tests, which may be a single item or task or a collection of items or tasks. These could be administered during class, on demand, or in the form of a take-home test to be completed outside of the classroom. And of course, this could include items or tasks administered online at any time.

Throughout the book, we are generally talking about tests and the practice of classroom testing. When we need to distinguish the broader assessment activities from testing, we explicitly use the term "assessment."

## Why Do Instructors Need to Know About Measurement and Testing?

Teachers and instructors conduct educational measurement and assessment on a regular basis. They select measurement tools, create measurement tools, administer and score measurement tools, use the results, and evaluate the quality of those tools. Moreover, educational measurement and testing provide important information that directly affects the futures of students in the grades they receive and the opportunities that grades provide them, including entering certain degree programs, accessing advanced courses, obtaining or retaining scholarships and fellowships, seeking admissions to graduate and professional school programs, obtaining teaching and research assistantships, and, in some fields, obtaining employment. Although it may not be apparent within a single course, grades based on test and assessment results have high-stakes implications for most students.

Susan Brookhart (2011) described the educational assessment knowledge and skills that are important for K–12 teachers, many of which apply to college instructors as well. She basically argued (in very clear language) that teachers should have some skills in the testing and assessment activities in which they engage on a regular basis. The knowledge and skills most relevant to college instructors include the following (slightly modified from Brookhart's article). College instructors should be able to:

1. understand how students learn in the content area they teach.
2. articulate learning objectives clearly that are consistent with the goals of the course, degree, department, and field that are attainable and assessable.
3. use multiple strategies for communicating what achievement of the learning objectives looks like.
4. understand the purposes and uses of multiple assessment strategies and have the skills to use them effectively.
5. analyze test questions and tasks so it is clear what knowledge, skills, and abilities students must have to respond successfully.
6. provide effective and useful assessment feedback to students.
7. score assessments to provide meaningful, appropriate, and useful information for decisions about students, including grading, to support student learning and development. This includes using assessment results to make decisions about course planning and program development.
8. use course-level achievement information to inform institutional assessment of student learning outcomes.
9. help students use assessment information to improve their learning strategies and make sound decisions about next steps, even beyond a particular course, in terms of their educational planning and progress.
10. carry out their legal and ethical responsibilities regarding their assessment practices.

See Brookhart (2011) for a deeper read of these points. In this book, we address many of these areas of knowledge and skill. Each chapter is structured around a set of learning objectives that clarify what you should know and be able to do as you proceed through the book. Learning objectives are listed at the beginning of each chapter, along with application exercises to check for learning.

> Ongoing efforts to improve our instructional practices are part of a professional responsibility and commitment to our students and colleagues, our programs and institutions, and our fields and professions.

For those instructors who are interested in exploring the literature on the scholarship of testing and assessment, we provide references to key articles throughout the book, emphasizing those that are more practical and accessible to the nonpsychometrician.

## Common Complaints About College Tests

There are many things to complain about in college and many things to praise. But uniformly, students are notorious for complaining about course tests. And to be honest, many of those complaints are well deserved. Some of these complaints include:

1.  The content of the test did not match the content covered in class.
2.  The questions cover facts that are too specific and detailed, not important concepts.
3.  The feedback provided does not help students understand their strengths and weaknesses or what students can do to improve their understanding.
4.  The questions are confusing and ambiguous, leading to items with no correct answer or multiple correct answers.
5.  There are trick questions on the test—where some distractors can be interpreted as right answers.
6.  The tests, combined, don't sufficiently assess the knowledge, skills, and abilities that are important for success in the class and beyond (e.g., major program or degree).

We've probably all heard these complaints in our classes—and many of us have made these same complaints in classes we've taken ourselves. We now have a chance to do something about it. We can transform our own practice, improving our item-writing and test-development skills. We have the opportunity to change student perceptions about tests and, ultimately, to use tests and assessments to improve our teaching and student learning.

## Organization of the Book

We have organized this book in a way to support your learning and skill development. Each chapter begins with a brief introduction, providing a summary of the contents of the chapter. This is followed by a short list of learning objectives, what we expect college instructors to know and be able to do from working through the chapter. Finally, we provide an opportunity for readers to practice the skills addressed in the chapter, with a few application tasks. We encourage you to try these application tasks yourself and continue to develop your own item-writing knowledge and skills. We acknowledge that teaching, assessment, and learning are inherently intertwined and that we can continue to develop our own practice while improving the learning outcomes and success of our students.

## Reference

Brookhart, S.M. (2011). Educational assessment knowledge and skills for teachers. *Educational Measurement: Issues and Practice*, 30(1), 3–12.

# 1 The Role of Testing in the College Classroom

In this chapter, we provide an introduction to validity, one that is used as a framework for the remainder of the book. Validity is the most important aspect of testing, as it provides the evidence needed to defend the intended interpretations and uses of test scores. Much of that validation can be established up front, through good item writing and test design and the alignment of test content to instructional learning objectives.

After describing the role of validity, we lay out a simple structure to draw attention to the purpose of assessment. We present common purposes of testing, with attention to potential uses of test results. We also note how this relates to grading and provide some research-based thoughts on grading. Finally, we review common methods of testing—as context for thinking about test design and item writing.

## Chapter Learning Objectives

1. Explain validity in terms of test score interpretation and use.
2. Provide examples of common uses of testing and how they support teaching and learning in the college classroom.
3. Describe the foundations of an effective grading plan, with details on how testing can inform grading.
4. Compare and contrast formative and summative uses of test results.
5. Summarize the forms of evidence that support validity.

## What Is Validity?

Formally, validity is the extent to which theory and evidence support the proposed interpretations and uses of test scores (AERA, APA, and NCME, 2014). This basically means that every proposed interpretation and use of a test score should be supported with evidence—which indicates that we have validity (evidence) to interpret and use test scores the way we intended.

Validation is the process of collecting that evidence—to support our interpretations and uses. We review a few ways to painlessly collect validity evidence below. It is important to realize that in collecting validity evidence, we can be more certain that the test results will improve teaching and learning appropriately, meaningfully, and usefully. Not to mention, grading will be fairer, that is, more likely to appropriately reflect achievement of course learning objectives.

## What Are Common Testing Purposes?

Although there are many different reasons or purposes for conducting tests, in the college classroom, there are a few key purposes. Above all, tests should measure the relevant knowledge, skills, and abilities (KSAs) students have achieved, as required in the course learning objectives. Important questions that can be answered by tests include:

1. Were my students prepared for the content demands in this course?
2. Are students achieving the course learning objectives?
3. What grades should students receive?
4. Are students prepared for more advanced courses?
5. Is my teaching supporting student learning?

KSAs are the knowledge, skills, and abilities we hope to develop in our students.

In classroom testing, the inferences and uses of test scores are focused on achievement of learning objectives (interpretation) and grading (use). We want to use test scores to make statements about what students know and can do. We need to make claims about our students' achievement of course learning objectives, so we test them to inform and support those claims.

Students also can ask questions about the results of tests that address their concerns:

1. Do I have the preparation it takes to succeed in this course?
2. Did I spend the right amount of effort and time to prepare for the test?
3. What do I need to study and where should I focus my learning efforts?
4. Am I ready for advanced study in this field?

Essentially, tests and all classroom assessments should support teaching and learning (and students' sense of their ability to learn). This claim leads to a coherent set of guidelines and recommendations throughout the book.

### A Note on Grading

We need information to use in grading student performance overall. The research on grading is clear, and we know that instructors often use non–achievement-related information to establish grades. College course grades should be clear and stable indicators of course achievement. Grades should also recognize growth, learning, and achievement at the end of the course. We should not punish students who start out with poor performance but by the end of the class clearly meet the learning objectives—for the purposes of improving achievement motivation but also to provide a more accurate indicator of the level of KSAs of our students.

Brookhart (2009) provided a thorough review of the research and evidence-based guidance on grading. In that review, she summarized a great deal of what we have learned through practice and research. Here are a few highlights:

- Grading practices were introduced first in higher education at least 400 years ago. From there, grading was introduced to K–12 schools during the common schools movement in the 1800s.
- By 1900, percentage grading (from 0 to 100) became common. In the 1910s, researchers showed how unreliable percentage grading was. Norm-referenced grading (such as grading on a curve) was a response to that criticism.
- Research in the 1920s and 1930s clearly demonstrated the problems with norm-referenced grading. They also found that instructors often used nonachievement factors including effort and attitude.
- From the 1930s to 1960s, educators turned their attention to improving learning, evaluating the achievement of learning objectives, and various forms of standards-based grading with reference to what students should know and be able to do.
- Shortly after 2000, especially with the focus on evaluating school performance relative to content standards, schools began using standards-based report cards (although still primarily in elementary schools).

We may also use test scores to inform our instruction: Is my teaching helping students understand core concepts? Similarly, we can use test scores and final grades to think more about a sequence of courses in a degree program. Did students have the prerequisite skills necessary to achieve in this course? Are students learning what will be needed in future or advanced courses? When we create tests that are primarily used to inform our instruction, it may not be fair to hold students accountable for their performance—especially if we aren't sure that our teaching or instruction is effective. Moreover, if tests early in the term are to be used to help students understand the demands and required KSAs to meet learning objectives, it may not be fair to hold them accountable for early performance. If the learning objectives are developed through the course of the term—where we continually work on deepening our understanding and ability to apply concepts in complex ways—then early performance is formative, and students are naturally expected to improve over time.

Grading systems are most effective in terms of promoting learning and increasing achievement motivation when they acknowledge that learning takes time. Grades should focus on the achievement of core learning objectives.

Grades should recognize the learning that students achieve and should reflect the learning process, acknowledging that students may not master the learning objectives until later in the course. Grades should communicate the level of mastery of the course learning objectives and provide some indication of how much students learned. Grades should not be overwhelmed by nonachievement factors, such as late assignments, attendance, participation, attitudes, and so on.

It is difficult for us to make recommendations on how other instructors should grade their students or what a grading policy should look like. Many colleges and universities, or at least departments and programs, have grading policies. But our experience is that such grading policies leave a lot of decisions up to the instructor. We can only reflect on the research around grading and provide advice based on what has been effective in other settings, much of which was summarized by Brookhart (2009). To that extent, we encourage you to adopt grading policies that recognize the importance of learning and progress and that define achievement in these terms, where mistakes are part of the learning process. Create a grading plan that does not incorporate lateness, attendance, participation, attitude, and other nonachievement factors, a grading plan that is clearly connected to the course learning objectives, one that values learning and gives more weight to performance later in the term. Grades shouldn't reflect time management or work habits; grades should reflect achievement. This will go a long way to promote learning in all students.

## What Are Common Uses of Test Results?

We need to make a distinction between two kinds of test use. One use is for formative purposes; the other is for summative purposes. You may have heard the phrase "formative assessment." It has become a major buzzword in K–12 education: "Data-driven decision making relies on formative assessments to improve teaching and learning." However, this is a bit of a misnomer. An assessment or test is not formative or summative, as these are not characteristics of tests themselves. These terms actually describe the uses of test results.

> Test results can be used for formative purposes, to inform instruction and learning, or for summative purposes, to evaluate performance and achievement, typically at the end of a unit or course.

### Formative Uses of Tests

To support and improve instruction and learning, test information can be used to evaluate how our teaching is progressing. We can answer questions like:

- Are the students understanding core concepts?
- Can students apply concepts in novel or more complex ways?
- Are my methods of instruction supporting student achievement?

When we see how our students are doing on each learning objective, we can use that information to take a number of actions:

- Review prerequisite knowledge to provide missing scaffolding for more complex concepts.
- Reteach a concept using multiple methods.
- Provide feedback to students so they know what they need to focus on or review.

From a large body of research on test use in classrooms, we know that testing matters in student learning. The effects of testing on student learning are substantial (Phelps, 2012). We strongly encourage you to take advantage of these effects and use test results to inform your teaching to support student learning—particularly in those areas where students have struggled (see Chapter 7 for more guidance on this).

### Summative Uses of Tests

In college classrooms, most of us are required to grade our students. We then seek ways to evaluate the extent to which students have achieved our learning objectives. We can elect to use tests for summative purposes. However, we caution you to restrict the summative uses of tests to the larger, more comprehensive tests, for example the final exam. After the final exam, we typically don't have a way to remediate teaching and learning. But students can use the final exam results to do a "final" evaluation of their strengths and weaknesses, particularly if this is important for preparing for the next course in a sequence— where the KSAs are prerequisite for later understanding and achievement.

We also caution you not to put a lot of weight on tests used for formative purposes—for supporting the learning process. If we haven't provided sufficient instruction, we shouldn't penalize students. Using tests for summative purposes is clearly important in college classrooms, and that practice should continue. But it should be done in such a way as to promote learning.

## What Are Common Methods of Testing?

The specific methods of testing have expanded greatly with the increased use of technology and online learning tools, whether the course is classroom based, online, or a hybrid. Because the number of such tools is so great, where many are developed in house, we do not review them here. But we recognize that tests can be developed and administered in many ways.

Paper–pencil tests are still common. These might include the 60-second brain-dump. You can hand out an index card (e.g., 3 × 5 card) and ask students, "List everything you know about validity in 60 seconds." Such tests can be reviewed quickly during class. Sometimes this can be done anonymously— which is true to the formative use of tests. We can use such information to do a quick check of students' understanding: Are we ready to move on?

You can pose questions during class using electronic devices or other class-room response systems. Students can pick up (or may keep during a term) a remote with a number of buttons that allows them to respond to questions posed by you during class. You can periodically project a question on the screen, ask students to respond with their remotes, then display the responses on the screen—providing immediate feedback (which we know enhances learning). When these questions are MC questions, they can quickly be answered and summarized multiple times during a lecture. But MC questions only inform teaching and learning if they are carefully constructed to measure relevant learning objectives.

Quizzes remain important tools for college instructors. They provide easy ways to periodically check student understanding and ability to apply con-cepts in novel settings. Quizzes can be administered out of class, in the online learning-management systems (e.g., Moodle, Blackboard). Quizzes can also be easily administered in class by posting questions on the board or via a projector (where students respond on paper), or of course on a paper–pencil test. There is evidence that more frequent, shorter tests are more valuable in terms of learn-ing than the typical midterm and final exams. Quizzes are often low-stakes tests that are used for formative purposes, so security is not a primary concern. Per-formance on such tests should be carefully considered before including them in final grades. If the quiz is really intended to be used for formative purposes, for example to ask the question: "Are students understanding the material so far?" then we may not want to hold students accountable for their performance— perhaps it is our cursory or introductory instruction that is inadequate. We may penalize our students for failing to learn content for which we have not yet adequately provided instruction or opportunities to learn.

Unit tests can be used for formative and summative purposes. There are points throughout a course at which we must reasonably expect students to have achieved some learning objectives. We must evaluate their achievement to provide grades but also to feel comfortable moving on in the course content. We can continue to provide feedback to ourselves (to inform instruction) and to our students (to support learning) as we evaluate student achievement of course learning objectives.

## How Do We Gather Validity Evidence?

The validity evidence we need to gather depends on the intended score inter-pretations and uses. But there is at least one common interpretation for nearly all classroom-based tests: Test scores provide information about what students know and can do relative to course learning objectives. This interpretation leads us to the intended use of test scores for grading purposes.

## Evidence About the Test Content

If we want to support an inference or test score interpretation to make claims about the achievement of learning objectives, then we need to gather evidence that the test does cover the relevant learning objectives. If we want to infer from test scores what students know and can do, then the test better include the relevant KSAs. If a unit exam will provide summative information about achievement regarding the content of a course unit, then the test better include a representative and balanced sample of the content covered in the unit. If the final exam is comprehensive, covering the key or core concepts of the entire course, then the test better cover the content of the course in an appropriate and balanced manner. If tests achieve these goals, then it is reasonable and fair to include the results of such tests in grading—as a summative measure of the achievement of course learning objectives.

One way to provide evidence that the right stuff is on the test is to create a test blueprint—which then guides us to develop items and tasks that appropriately cover the relevant content and requisite KSAs. Chapter 3 covers the process of developing a test blueprint with examples. But first, Chapter 2 introduces and briefly explains the role of learning objectives, with some guidance in developing learning objectives. Learning objectives are an important means for creating a test blueprint and thus are an important component of validation.

## Evidence About the Quality of Test Items

Another form of validity evidence supports the use of scores, in that the scores are sound or based on high-quality information from item responses. Basically, we need to provide some evidence that the test questions are good enough to use the response to each question to contribute to the total score. This then means that the test questions themselves are good measurement tools. This is the focus of this book!

How do we know that test questions are of high enough quality or good enough to include in the total score? There are lots of technical approaches to evaluating test item quality, few of which work in the context of college classrooms. Many methods require large samples. But most colleges and universities have an office that provides measurement services to instructors, with test scoring and reporting services. These reporting services provide item statistics that can be used to judge the quality of test items, including item difficulty, item discrimination, and distractor frequencies. Such reports also include information about overall test score quality in the form of test score reliability.

These methods of item and test score analyses are described more completely in Chapter 7. When we are able to obtain item statistics, we can make decisions about retaining or revising items for future use—improving our item-writing ability and test-design skills overall. These are useful practices for all college instructors.

### Other Forms of Evidence

Other forms of validity evidence are more appropriate for large-scale testing or high-stakes testing, such as certification or licensure tests, graduation tests, or admissions tests. These methods are referred to as criterion-related validity evidence and construct-related validity evidence. For classroom tests, where the key interpretations and uses have to do with achievement of learning objectives, the most important evidence addresses the extent to which the test has the right content (often called content-related validity evidence). For a deep read on the current thinking about validity and validation, see Michael Kane's (2013) applied article in *School Psychology Review*. Kane has synthesized decades of theoretical and practical work in validation and succinctly presented it in a framework based on the idea of validation as argument, so that we no longer collect validity evidence for the sake of validity but in a targeted way to support the claims we intend to make from test scores.

## How Do We Engage Students?

A key to successful teaching and learning is understanding the connection between the content of the course, the learning objectives of the course, and the background and preparation of students, including the recognition of the ways of knowing and ways of doing in the field and among the students. We struggle in some fields with a history of limited diversity, particularly in professions related to STEM (science, technology, engineering, and mathematics) fields. Because of the limited diversity in the historical development of some fields, ways of knowing and ways of doing are also limited. By recognizing diverse ways of knowing and doing, we all can benefit from previously untapped approaches and undiscovered advancements. When we recognize the backgrounds and experiences of our students, we can link those experiences to the subject matter in important ways that will surely improve student engagement—giving every student a reason to learn beyond "because it's required."

Assessments provide an important means for us to engage students in the subject matter and potentially explore professions in fields that have been traditionally less diverse. Bill Mehrens and Irv Lehmann (1991), both past presidents of the National Council on Measurement in Education, regularly made the following argument, with which we agree whole heartedly:

> *Students learn while preparing for the test, while taking the test, and while reviewing the test.*

The message is that tests are important and they matter. In many cases, the clearest message of what is important in a class or what is valued in the subject matter or field is what shows up on the test. If the wrong stuff appears on the test, students receive the wrong messages of what is important and valued. But if a student's experiences, background, and ways of knowing and doing are never reflected on the test, an implicit message is that they are not valued or relevant to the subject matter, field, or profession. This is an unfortunate and hopefully unintended message.

As college instructors, we have the opportunity to bring untapped perspectives and innovative ways of knowing and doing to our subject areas, our fields, and our professions. We can do this by getting to know our students and recognizing how diverse experiences and perspectives relate to the subject matter through our instruction and assessment practices. We can create assessment activities and write test items in the many diverse contexts of our students, connecting them in important ways to the content. If nothing else, we can recognize that there are potentially innovative ways of knowing and doing in our subject areas—it is what drives our commitment to continually learning about our fields.

> We can inspire commitment to learning in our students by continually improving our instruction and assessment practices.

## Applications

This chapter summarizes validity as it pertains to the formative and summative uses of testing in the college classroom. Examples are provided of valid uses of test scores to inform teaching and instruction, promote learning, and support grading. In the following exercises, you will apply what you learned in this chapter by reflecting on how you use assessment in your classroom.

1. Examine the different ways you use assessment in your classroom. Are these formative or summative uses of assessment? Do you have the right mix at the right times of the term?
2. Evaluate the grading plan for your course. Does your plan incorporate variables unrelated to achievement? Does it rely on tests used for formative and summative purposes? Does it account for learning?
3. Review the validity evidence supporting each of your tests. Does this evidence justify the way test scores are used? Are your tests representative of the content they are intended to cover?
4. Consider how your students interact with your tests. Do they find your tests engaging and representative of learning and achievement? Is your test content relevant to your students, given their diverse backgrounds?

# References

American Educational Research Association, American Psychological Association, and National Council on Education in Measurement. (2014). *Standards for educational and psychological testing*. Washington, DC: American Educational Research Association.

Brookhart, S. M. (2009). *Grading* (2nd ed.). Upper Saddle River, NJ: Pearson Education.

Kane, M. (2013). The argument-based approach to validation. *School Psychology Review, 42*(2), 448–457.

Phelps, R. P. (2012). The effect of testing on student achievement, 1910–2010. *International Journal of Testing, 12*, 21–43.

# 2    The Role of Learning
Objectives

In this chapter, we introduce the basic structure and functions of institutional, course, and instructional learning objectives. We discuss broad and generic learning objectives and demonstrate how to turn these into meaningful, appropriate, and useful objectives that will lead to effective test item development. We also provide example objectives from different fields.

### Chapter Learning Objectives

1. Explain the similarities and differences between objectives written at the institutional, course, and instructional levels.
2. Describe how instructional learning objectives are used to support teaching and learning.
3. Identify and provide examples of the six levels of cognitive tasks (remember, understand, apply, analyze, evaluate, and create).
4. Evaluate the quality of instructional learning objectives.
5. Create effective instructional learning objectives that specify student performances, conditions under which they are completed, and criteria by which they are evaluated for a given topic and cognitive task.

## Where Do Learning Objectives Fit In?

The key to effective testing in any context is clearly identifying the purpose of the test and ensuring that each item supports that purpose. For classroom assessment, the purpose is almost always to evaluate students' subject-matter KSAs (knowledge, skills, and abilities). In short, classroom tests should provide information to instructors and students about what students have learned. Unfortunately, in many classes, the learning objectives are either nonexistent or are too general or broad to be useful and supportive of item writing.

Learning objectives are sometimes called learning outcomes, learning expectations, learning or teaching targets, and other related terms—there are no real differences between these concepts. Some might argue that one emphasizes certain components over the others. How we use them is more important than what we call them.

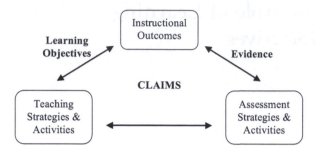

*Figure 2.1* A Common Model of Instruction and Assessment

Learning objectives allow us to be systematic about gathering assessment evidence of academic achievement for the purposes of improving student learning and our teaching.

- Learning Objectives: What are the claims we want to make about our students?
- Valued Evidence: What can our students do to demonstrate their knowledge, skills, and abilities?
- Using Results: How can we use this evidence to inform our teaching and student learning?

## What Is a Learning Objective?

Learning objectives are simple but specific statements that define the expected goals or purposes of instruction. College and university courses may have a number of purposes, but most often, we teach to develop the KSAs of our students—to advance understanding of the subject matter. Other purposes might exist, but these are also often related to advancing understanding of the subject matter, for example:

- To meet general or degree requirements (one option of several),
- To prepare students for advanced courses (serves as a prerequisite),
- To prepare students for graduate or professional programs,
- To prepare students for success in a profession,
- To provide students opportunities to explore personal interests (electives, not required).

Each of these broad purposes is based on learning the subject matter.

Regardless of the purpose of the course or the reasons why students take it, every course must define learning objectives and they should be communicated in the syllabus.

At colleges and universities, there are at least three levels of objectives to contend with. There are institutional learning objectives, typically called student learning outcomes. There are also broad learning objectives for courses, hopefully just a few. Then there are more specific learning objectives that focus instruction and learning in units or major sections of a course, typically called instructional learning objectives.

### Institutional Learning Outcomes

Accreditation of institutions of higher education requires evidence of student learning outcomes. The institutional-level student learning outcomes provide institutionwide direction and communicate the major claims being made about what students can expect from their education at that institution. They also promote consistency and focus across departments. Institutional learning outcomes are achieved over longer periods of time, typically meaning a year or more of study.

Across the country, these institutional learning outcomes are fairly similar. Most colleges and universities have learning outcomes that address writing skills, critical thinking, quantitative reasoning skills, oral communication skills, and subject-matter knowledge (Hart Research Associates, 2016). At the University of Minnesota (2015), for example, there are seven learning outcomes. They are described in this way:

> At the time of receiving a bachelor's degree, students:
> * Can identify, define, and solve problems.
> * Can locate and critically evaluate information.
> * Have mastered a body of knowledge and a mode of inquiry.
> * Understand diverse philosophies and cultures within and across societies.
> * Can communicate effectively.
> * Understand the role of creativity, innovation, discovery, and expression across disciplines.
> * Have acquired skills for effective citizenship and lifelong learning.

### Course-Level Learning Objectives

To promote high-quality instruction and support high levels of learning and achievement, it is critical to articulate the learning objectives of each course. Course learning objectives are tailored to the specific course and provide guides for planning the major units of instruction and communicate what a student should expect from their participation in the course. They also demonstrate how the course helps achieve the institutional student learning outcomes. Course objectives are achieved as a result of completing the requirements for the course.

These are the statements that articulate what students are expected to learn in a course, what students who complete the course should know and be able to do, as declared in the syllabus. In some cases, these are called learning goals because they are broadly stated but specific to a course. A course should only have 5 to 10 major learning objectives. Effective course learning objectives:

1.   Are student centered,
2.   Are observable,
3.   Address important and core content.

> It is critical to recognize that regardless of the purpose of the course or the reasons why students take them, every instructor must define learning objectives and clearly communicate them in the syllabus.

### Instructional Learning Objectives

Instructional learning objectives are more specific and descriptive, outlining the key components of a unit or section of a course. They can help guide the development of a lesson plan or at least provide an outline for lessons, lectures, activities, assignments, and class discussions. Instructional learning objectives are achieved as the result of a single class session or some combination of class sessions and activities or experiences.

Within most courses, there are units or sections that are more focused in terms of the content covered. Each unit or major section of the course should have its own learning objectives. Instructional learning objectives provide guidance for developing a test blueprint (described in what follows) and provide the targets for writing test items. Multiple test items can be written to address each objective. In addition to the characteristics of course-level learning objectives, instructional learning objectives should be:

1.   Behavioral,
2.   Measureable,
3.   Attainable.

## What Are Effective Learning Objectives?

Next we describe characteristics of effective learning objectives, as well as show examples of poor learning objectives. But our focus is on providing guidance to create high-quality objectives that support teaching and learning. Effective learning objectives:

* Reflect current thinking and expectations of the field and subject-matter experts,
* Publically and clearly communicate what students need to know and be able to do,

- Convey the important and essential aspects of the course content and how learning progresses throughout the course,
- Help students focus their study behaviors,
- Help instructors focus instruction,
- Help instructors develop appropriate assessment activities and exam items,
- Provide information to instructors about the effectiveness of their instruction,
- Provide information to students about the effectiveness of their learning efforts,
- Support student self-reflection and self-assessment.

When we begin developing effective learning objectives for a typical course, there are a number of things to consider. Course objectives should be limited to a small number for the course overall and for each unit. Objectives should focus on important aspects of the subject matter—core KSAs. They should be phrased using student-centered statements and should address learning that results from participation in the course while acknowledging alternative pathways to learning and performance. Finally, they should be sensitive to instruction, reflecting what we hope to claim as a result of instruction.

## Why Are Common Generic Learning Objectives Less Useful?

The novice instructor tends to write learning objectives that are generic, too broad, and not measurable. We often see objectives such as the following:

Students will . . .
- learn effective communication strategies.
- appreciate diverse art forms.
- be able to use quadratic equations.
- have the opportunity to analyze real patient histories.
- explore the origins of the universe.
- demonstrate an understanding of reliability.

Hopefully you notice that these statements are vague, without context, not directly connected to course content, or, in some cases, not outcomes ("have the opportunity" or "explore"). Moreover, these statements do not contain observable behaviors or state the performance students will demonstrate. These statements are not helpful to the instructor that needs to write test items. Mostly, it is not clear what the student will do (missing action verbs), and the statements provide no criteria for knowing whether the student has achieved the outcome (not measurable). It's very difficult (if not impossible) to see "learn" or "appreciate" in a way that allows us to evaluate it.

Verbs that are often used in generic and vague learning objectives include:

- know,
- understand,
- appreciate,
- learn,
- believe.

These verbs should not be used when writing effective learning objectives.

## What Are Cognitive Tasks?

Learning objectives typically refer to different types of cognitive tasks. The most common taxonomy of cognitive tasks is the one proposed by Benjamin Bloom and colleagues (1956). The Bloom taxonomy of objectives includes six levels of cognitive tasks.

1. Knowledge: Remember facts, definitions of terms, principles, procedures.
2. Comprehension: Understand the meaning of material, reasons, and roles of principles or practices.
3. Application: Problem solve, apply material in novel contexts, including concepts, principles, rules.
4. Analysis: Decompose concepts, identify parts and their roles, relations among principles, make inferences or draw conclusions, organize, determine why.
5. Synthesis: Combine elements or principles in unique ways, create new principles or patterns.
6. Evaluation: Judge the value of an argument, use criteria for decision making.

Bloom argued that there is a hierarchy in these objectives, in that lower objectives must be met in order to achieve higher objectives. However, evidence of this hierarchy has been limited, with rigorous challenges to its existence (Ormell, 1974; Phillips and Kelly, 1975). In terms of item writing to tap various objectives, it is difficult for content experts to classify a given item in the same way as the item writer intended—beyond knowledge, comprehension, and application, the objectives are difficult to replicate or validate in item writing (Cox, 1965; Stanley and Bolton, 1957).

More recently, a group of educational researchers revised the original Bloom's cognitive levels into language that fits classroom learning expectations more practically. The six cognitive tasks are defined as follows (Anderson and Krathwohl, 2001, pp. 67–68):

1. Remember: Retrieve relevant knowledge from long-term memory.
2. Understand: Construct meaning from instructional messages, including oral, written, and graphic communication.

3. Apply: Carry out or use procedure in a given situation.
4. Analyze: Break material into its constituent parts and determine how the parts relate to one another and to an overall structure or purpose.
5. Evaluate: Make judgments based on criteria and standards.
6. Create: Put elements together to form a coherent or functional whole; reorganize elements into a new pattern or structure.

This structure for cognitive tasks makes sense to us and has been applied in all subject areas. Of course, some cognitive tasks are more important in some courses than others—which is the beauty of developing and selecting learning objectives. They should be tailored to your course.

We also recognize that there is increasing complexity in the cognitive processes from remembering to creating, but not an absolute hierarchy. In addition, this also maps to the challenge in developing strong selected-response (SR) or MC items. It is certainly easier to develop MC items that tap memory and recall; it is substantially more challenging to develop MC items that tap the ability to create—although not impossible! Often, a series of well-constructed MC items can mimic complex processes, like creating, shaping, or reorganizing. But if you're looking for novel or innovative creating, MC items are probably not the best option—constructed-response and performance tasks will provide more direct measurement of such skills.

We encourage you to develop learning objectives that quickly move students beyond remembering to tap higher-order cognitive processes. This will give you a structure to develop test items that also tap more important cognitive skills. But such learning objectives and test items must provide students with opportunities to demonstrate these skills, so that students **cannot** answer test items through memory alone.

### Cognitive Tasks and Processes

In the description of the cognitive tasks by Lorin Anderson and David Krathwohl (2001), each cognitive task is associated with a number of cognitive processes. Cognitive processes break down each task into a set of observable and measurable behaviors. Example cognitive processes follow each task:

1. Remember: Recognizing, recalling
2. Understand: Interpreting, exemplifying, classifying, summarizing, inferring, comparing, explaining
3. Apply: Executing, implementing
4. Analyze: Differentiating, organizing, attributing
5. Evaluate: Checking, critiquing
6. Create: Generating, planning, producing

## How Do We Construct Learning Objectives?

One approach to developing learning objectives that has received attention and appreciation by K–12 educators was proposed by Robert Mager (1997). Mager introduced three parts of effective performance-based learning objectives:

1. A performance (what the student does),
2. Conditions (under which the student performs),
3. Criteria (by which the performance is evaluated).

A model can be used to create learning objectives for most courses:

State the content-relevant topic:

- Specify the performance, what the student will do (action verb)
- Specify the conditions under which the student performs
- Specify the criteria by which the performance is evaluated

Topic: *Norm-referenced and criterion-referenced testing*

- Performance: *distinguish (select from, match, or sort)*
- Conditions: *five common score interpretations*
- Criteria: *four out of five (or all)*

The resulting learning objective: *The student will correctly distinguish four out of the five common score interpretations and their appropriateness for norm-referenced versus criterion-referenced testing.*

The content-relevant topic: _____

- Performance: _____
- Conditions: _____
- Criteria: _____

Teaching and learning centers at a variety of colleges and universities suggest making these statements more consistent and direct, setting high yet attainable expectations. For example, guidance from the Office of Medical Education at Boston University School of Medicine (2005) suggests that for most classroom tests, the conditions for student learning include course lectures, activities, readings, and other opportunities described in the course syllabus. Also, the criteria should be a consistent expectation of 100% correct, that the student should, with appropriate learning opportunities, learn the content.

### A General Model for College Course Learning Objectives

We offer a general model for course-level learning objectives that can be refined and tailored for individual courses. In addition, these can be made more specific for each unit within a course.

The content-relevant topic: _____

- Performance: [*action verb*] _____
- Conditions: *learning opportunities described in the syllabus* _____
- Criteria: *100% correct performance* _____

An example learning objective: *Students will correctly classify five common test score interpretations as appropriate for norm-referenced or criterion-referenced testing.*

Finally, the best guidance for developing learning objectives consistently recommends the use of concrete, measurable, action verbs. There are lots of lists of action verbs available online.

### Sample Online Guides for Developing Learning Objectives and Tests

There are many resources online for developing effective learning objectives. Most colleges and universities with offices of teaching and learning offer online guidance for everything from course design to writing learning objectives to developing course assessments and tests. Check with your college or university to see what supports are offered for instructors. Here is a sample of the resources available at U.S. colleges and universities.

*Table 2.1* Online Guides for Developing Learning Objectives and Tests

| Center name and location | Center URL |
| --- | --- |
| Center for Teaching & Learning, Brigham Young University | http://ctl.byu.edu/ |
| Center for Educational Innovation, University of Minnesota | http://cei.umn.edu/support-services/tutorials/integrated-aligned-course-design |
| Center for Teaching, Vanderbilt University | https://cft.vanderbilt.edu/teaching-guides/reflecting-and-assessing/ |
| Center for Teaching & Learning, University of North Carolina, Charlotte | http://teaching.uncc.edu/learning-resources/articles-books/best-practice/assessment-grading |
| Center for Teaching & Learning, UC Berkeley | http://teaching.berkeley.edu/resources/improve |
| College of Medicine, The University of Arizona | http://fid.medicine.arizona.edu/sites/default/files/u4/writing_goals_and_objectives_packet.pdf |
| College of Medicine, Florida State University | http://med.fsu.edu/index.cfm?page=facultydevelopment.behavobjectives |
| Eberly Center of Teaching Excellence & Educational Innovation, Carnegie-Mellon University | www.cmu.edu/teaching/designteach/design/learningobjectives.html |

(Continued)

*Table 2.1* (Continued)

| Center name and location | Center URL |
| --- | --- |
| Faculty Innovation Center, University of Texas at Austin | http://facultyinnovate.utexas.edu/teaching/assess-learning |
| Mountain View College, Dallas County Community College District | http://ctl.tedu.edu.tr/sites/default/files/content_files/docs/instructional_objectives.pdf |
| Office of Planning & Assessment, Texas Tech University | www.depts.ttu.edu/opa/resources/docs/Writing_Learning_Outcomes_Handbook3.pdf |
| Office of Teaching, Learning, & Technology, University of Iowa | https://teach.its.uiowa.edu/resources/collections/assessment |
| Schreyer Institute for Teaching Excellence, Penn State University | www.schreyerinstitute.psu.edu/tools/popular.aspx |
| Assessment Resources for Science, Technology, Engineering, & Mathematics; National Institute for Science Education, University of Wisconsin-Madison | www.flaguide.org/resource/websites.php |

*Table 2.2* Cognitive Tasks and Associated Action Verbs

| Cognitive task | Action verbs |
| --- | --- |
| 1. Remember | Arrange, choose, define, identify, label, list, match, name, recognize, repeat, reproduce, select, state, underline |
| 2. Understand | Associate, defend, describe, explain, extend, generalize, give examples, identify, locate, predict, restate, rewrite, summarize |
| 3. Apply | Apply, assign, calculate, classify, complete, employ, execute, illustrate, interpret, modify, respond, solve, translate, use, utilize |
| 4. Analyze | Arrange, break down, categorize, combine, detect, diagram, differentiate, discriminate, infer, relate, separate, solve |
| 5. Evaluate | Appraise, assess, compare, conclude, contrast, critique, estimate, interpret, judge, justify, measure, rank, rate |
| 6. Create | Categorize, combine, compile, construct, devise, explain, modify, order, predict, propose, rearrange, recommend, reorganize, revise, transform |

Effective learning objectives are written with action verbs, making them behavioral, observable, and measurable. Here is a sample of the kinds of verbs that are appropriate for each cognitive task (Table 2.2).

Many of these action verbs can be used for multiple cognitive tasks, given the nature of the learning objective. The cognitive tasks are also permeable—when it comes to learning behaviors, many behaviors include aspects of multiple cognitive tasks.

**Example Learning Objectives**

Next we provide example learning objectives at multiple levels with different degrees of specificity from a variety of fields. These include institutional, course, and instructional learning objectives.

*Accounting*

Canisius College, Buffalo, NY, provides online access to course-level learning objectives (which they call goals) and instructional objectives for most classes. Here are two course goals and objectives for an accounting course (www. canisius.edu/ugrad-accounting/). These objectives will support the development of test items.

Students will:
- Apply current principles of accounting to the measurement and reporting of accounting information.
    o Construct the financial statements in accordance with generally accepted accounting principles and analyze the strengths and weaknesses of each statement;
    o Evaluate the reporting and valuation of assets and liabilities in accordance with generally accepted accounting principles;
    o Evaluate the various alternatives to the measurement of income and the determination of financial position.

- Know how to compare/contrast alternative business decisions and evaluate the potential impact of these decisions on future financial performance.
    o Demonstrate a sound understanding of cost behavior and analyze the differences resulting from fixed and variable costs in financial performance;
    o Analyze the differences that result in financial reporting from the company's choice of inventory costing techniques;
    o Apply budgeting techniques in the preparation of static and flexible budgets.

*Biology*

Also from Canisius College, another set of sample goals and objectives was drawn in biology (http://catalog.canisius.edu/undergraduate/college-arts-sciences/biology/#learninggoalstext), including these two course goals and objectives.

Students will:
- Develop competency with respect to knowledge, having a working understanding of basic concepts in the biological sciences.
    o Demonstrate detailed knowledge within at least two areas of biology to be selected among the following: from ecology/

> evolutionary biology; molecular biology/cellular biology/bio-chemistry; physiology/organism biology;
> o  Connect previously learned material with current research in biology.

- Develop problem-solving skills applicable to the biological sciences.
  - o  Accurately interpret data;
  - o  Design an experiment to address a specific hypothesis;
  - o  Critically analyze an article from the original scientific literature or a professional report.

### College Calculus

City College of San Francisco provides an online listing of its mathematics department courses, with course outlines each including course learning objectives (www.ccsf.edu/en/educational-programs/school-and-departments/school-of-science-and-mathematics/mathematics/courses.html). The first five learning objectives for the course Calculus I (Math 110A) include the following.

> Upon completion of this course, students will be able to:
> - Describe, graph, compare, and contrast polynomial, rational, algebraic, trigonometric, and exponential functions and their inverses.
> - Define and interpret the concepts of limit, continuity, and derivative of a function verbally, algebraically, and graphically.
> - Evaluate limits of functions.
> - Interpret the derivative of a number in multiple ways, including slope of a tangent line and instantaneous rate of change.
> - Calculate derivatives of a wide variety of functions obtained by applying transformations, algebraic operations, and compositions to the families of functions mentioned in outcome A (the first outcome in this list).

### Discrete Mathematics

Also from City College of San Francisco, we pulled the learning outcomes from their course on Discrete Mathematics (Math 115). Examples of the major learning outcomes include the following.

> Upon completion of this course, students will be able to:
> - Analyze essential features of algorithms, especially time complexity.
> - Apply mathematical induction to construct mathematical proofs, to establish program correctness, and to solve problems involving recursion.

- Define and apply relations of sets, including equivalence relations, partial orderings, and functions.
- Use graph theory to analyze networking, matching problems, and optimization problems.

### Educational and Psychological Measurement

Course objectives for the introductory measurement course at the University of Minnesota (www.edmeasurement.net/5221/) are described in the following way.

Students who complete this course will be able to
- Assist in the development of measures of educational and psychological characteristics, attributes, or traits;
- Evaluate measures of educational and psychological constructs;
- Design and conduct validation studies;
- Interpret test and assessment scores from a variety of sources;
- Apply principles of measurement for responsible and fair test use.

### Measurement and Evaluation in Education and Psychology

Here is a set of instructional objectives for a course in educational and psychological measurement for a unit on reliability (modified from Mehrens and Lehmann, 1991).

After studying this chapter, students should be able to:
- Classify sources of error variance in educational and psychological measurement.
- Define the theoretical components of reliability, including associations between true score and observed score variance.
- Derive the standard error of measurement from the theoretical reliability formula.
- Interpret score bands reflecting the standard error of measurement.
- Describe the differences among different estimates of reliability.
- Identify factors that influence reliability estimates and the nature of the influence.

### Geology

Truman College has a system of general education goals, which provides structure for course learning objectives. Physical Science 111 (http://justonly .com/physci/ps111/learning_outcomes.php) includes the following instructional objectives for the units on geology.

At the completion of this course, the successful student will be able to do the following:

- Differentiate between minerals and rocks and identify many of the common rocks.
- Classify types of rocks and draw the rock cycle.
- List causative agents and products of various types of erosion.
- Describe the causes and results of diastrophism.
- Classify earthquake waves, faults, and types of unconformities.
- Sort and identify a mixture of minerals according to their physical properties.
- Identify geological land forms and describe their origin.
- Relate diastrophism and land forms to tectonic plate motion.

### Managing Chronic Pain

From the Langone Medical Center, NY, University School of Medicine (www.med.nyu.edu/cme/sites/default/files/cme/Examples_of_Well-Written_Learning_Objectives.pdf), a course objective (relatively general) is followed by two instructional objectives (more specific).

Students will develop the ability to:
- Manage chronic pain in the patient with risk factors for cardiovascular and/or gastrointestinal complications.
  - List two stages in peripheral sensitization that lead to central sensitization of pain as part of the acute-to-chronic pain scenario.
  - Identify two pharmacologic and two nonpharmacologic treatments for low-back pain in the patient with underlying cardiovascular gastrointestinal disease.

### Migraine Treatment

Also from the Langone Medical Center, NY, University School of Medicine (www.med.nyu.edu/cme/sites/default/files/cme/Examples_of_Well-Written_Learning_Objectives.pdf), a course objective (relatively general) is an example from a course on pain management.

Students will develop the ability to:
- Tailor the treatment of migraines to meet the needs of your patient.
  - Identify at least one screening tool that can help increase the accurate identification of patients with migraine.
  - Choose two agents, based on an approach of stratified care, which should be used from the outset in a patient with disabling migraine.

## Medicine

Boston University School of Medicine (2014) created a set of institutional learning objectives that can be summarized in the acronym BU CARES. They have also linked these institutional objectives to the competencies from the Accreditation Council for Graduate Medical Education (these are identified in parentheses).

- Behaves in a caring, compassionate, and sensitive manner toward patients and colleagues of all cultures and backgrounds (Patient Care and Professionalism)
- Uses the science of normal and abnormal states of health to prevent disease, to recognize and diagnose illness, and to provide an appropriate level of care (Medical Knowledge; Patient Care)
- Communicates with colleagues and patients to ensure effective interprofessional medical care (Interpersonal and Communication Skills, Patient Care)
- Acts in accordance with the highest ethical standards of medical practice (Professionalism)
- Reviews and critically appraises biomedical literature and evidence for the purpose of ongoing improvement of the practice of medicine (Practice-based Learning and Improvement, Medical Knowledge)
- Exhibits commitment and aptitude for lifelong learning and continuing improvement as a physician (Practice-based Learning)
- Supports optimal patient care through identifying and using resources of the health care system (Systems-based Practice; Patient Care)

## Music Appreciation

In the context of a course on music appreciation (fictional), we can conceive of a set of general learning objectives.

Upon successful completion of this course, students should be able to:
- Distinguish among the characteristics of the renaissance, baroque, classical, and romantic periods.
- Identify the sounds of different instruments and instrumental families.
- Relate how the use of different musical elements contributes to the aesthetic appeal of a work.
- Describe the characteristics of the four instrumental groupings of an orchestra.

These learning objectives can be improved by tailoring them to specific course content, given the materials covered at the time of the test. For example, the first unit test may include the first two historical musical style periods, and the first learning objective can be specified to distinguish certain kinds of characteristics (instruments used, complexity of compositions, dynamics, form, etc.) of those two periods. This could be the basis for a set of items that are in true-false or either-or format (described later), where the student must state whether each characteristic is typical of one or the other or both periods.

### APA Psychology Major Goals and Learning Outcomes

The American Psychological Association (2013) has articulated five global learning goals to provide uniformity across programs and institutions preparing undergraduate psychology majors. These five goal areas are broad and global. The goals are:

Goal 1: Knowledge Base in Psychology
Goal 2: Scientific Inquiry and Critical Thinking
Goal 3: Ethical and Social Responsibility in a Diverse World
Goal 4: Communication
Goal 5: Professional Development

Within each global goal area, a number of learning outcomes are provided that employ action verbs and are intended to be measurable. Within each learning outcome, several "indicators" for achieving the outcomes are provided as examples. These indicators are provided for students completing foundational psychology courses as well as those who have completed baccalaureate degrees in psychology. Examples of these levels of objectives for foundational psychology courses are summarized here (APA, 2013).

*Goal 1: Knowledge Base in Psychology*

Learning outcome 1.3: Describe applications of psychology

1.3a   Describe examples of relevant and practical applications of psychological principles to everyday life.
1.3b   Summarize psychological factors that can influence the pursuits of a healthy lifestyle.
1.3c   Correctly identify antecedents and consequences of behavior and mental processes.

*Goal 2: Scientific Inquiry and Critical Thinking*

Learning outcome 2.1: Use scientific reasoning to interpret psychological phenomena

2.1a   Identify basic biological, psychological, and social components of psychological explanations (e.g., inferences, observations, operational definitions, interpretations).
2.1c   Use an appropriate level of complexity to interpret behavior and mental processes.
2.1d   Ask relevant questions to gather more information about behavioral claims.

These objectives are not intended to be specific course learning objectives and are not specific enough to provide clear guidance for item development, but they provide an excellent collection of learning goals and objectives that can be tailored to meet the specific expectations for many psychology courses. In addition to these indicators, APA provides some guidance for test development:

> Test questions about research methods and critical thinking must be carefully constructed to produce distracters that represent flawed reasoning. However, lower level objectives that concentrate on acquiring scientific terminology can reasonably be addressed with objective testing. Strategies that require students to identify flaws in research design can also be useful in assessing reasoning and knowledge of methods.
>
> (APA, 2013, p. 23)

We present approaches to achieve these recommendations, with examples and guidance to develop the skills to improve our course tests and exams.

- Learning objectives: Are the student learning objectives written in measurable terms?
- Valued evidence: What indicators are valued to be considered meaningful evidence of the learning objectives?
- Assessment tools: What existing or new assessments are needed to gather relevant evidence?

## Applications

This chapter compares institutional, course, and instructional learning objectives and then describes in detail the process of writing instructional learning objectives to support student achievement of KSAs. An effective instructional learning objective is behavioral, measureable, and attainable, and it clearly addresses an instructional topic in terms of a specific cognitive task, so as to identify the conditions and criteria used to evaluate student performance. In the activities that follow, you will apply what you learned in this chapter by evaluating some example objectives and then creating/revising and evaluating objectives for your own course.

1. Review the example geology objectives presented in this chapter. For each objective, identify the cognitive task involved and the features that make the objective behavioral and measureable.
2. Evaluate the learning objectives for this chapter. Do they include the key features that we've recommended? Would they be effective in a course on item writing and test development?
3. Revise or create new course objectives and then instructional learning objectives for your course. Ask a peer to review them and provide feedback.
4. Compare your course objectives with your college or university institutional objectives. Do they align and support one another?

# References

American Psychological Association. (2013). *APA guidelines for the undergraduate psychology major: Version 2.0.* Washington, DC: Author. Retrieved at www.apa.org/ed/precollege/undergrad

Anderson, L. W., and Krathwohl, D. R. (Eds.) (2001). *A taxonomy of learning, teaching, and assessment: A revision of Bloom's taxonomy of educational objectives.* New York, NY: Longman. Retrieved at http://tinyurl.com/AndersonKrathwohl2001

Bloom, B. S. (Ed.) (1956). *Taxonomy of educational objectives: The classification of educational goals. Book 1: Cognitive domain* (2nd ed.). New York, NY: Longman.

Boston University School of Medicine. (2005). *An easy way to write learning objectives.* Boston, MA: Author, Office of Medical Education. Retrieved at www.bumc.bu.edu/busm/files/2016/01/ocs-easy-way-to-write-learning-objectives.pdf

Boston University School of Medicine. (2014). *The BU CARES institutional learning objectives.* Boston, MA: Author, Office of Medical Education. Retrieved at www.bumc.bu.edu/busm/files/2015/06/BUCARES.pdf

Cox, R. C. (1965). Item selection techniques and evaluation of instructional objectives. *Journal of Educational Measurement, 2*(2), 181–185.

Hart Research Associates. (2016). *Trends in learning outcomes assessment.* Association of American Colleges & Universities. Retrieved at www.aacu.org/about/2015-membersurvey

Mager, R. F. (1997). *Preparing instructional objectives.* Atlanta, GA: The Center for Effective Performance, Inc.

Mehrens, W. A., and Lehmann, I. J. (1991). *Measurement and evaluation in education and psychology* (4th ed.). Orlando, FL: Harcourt Brace Jovanovich.

Ormell, C. P. (1974). Bloom's taxonomy and the objectives of education. *Educational Research, 17,* 3–18.

Phillips, D. C., and Kelly, M. E. (1975). Hierarchical theories of development in education and psychology. *Harvard Educational Review, 45,* 351–375.

Stanley, J. C., and Bolton, D. T. (1957). A review of Bloom's "Taxonomy of educational objectives" and J. R. Gerberick's "Specimen objective test items, a guide to achievement test construction." *Educational and Psychological Measurement, 17,* 631–634.

University of Minnesota. (2015). *Student learning outcomes: Student learning, outcomes assessment, and accreditation.* Minneapolis, MN: Author. Retrieved at http://academic.umn.edu/provost/teaching/Uslo07.pdf

# 3   Planning the Quiz or Test

With a syllabus outlining the content of your course, where effective learning objectives have been clearly stated, you have the basic building blocks of a quiz or test. In this chapter, we introduce a framework for building a test blueprint, which serves as an item-writing guide allowing you to write items that produce a test with the right balance of content and intended cognitive tasks. Test blueprints lay out the basic structure of the test, including the types of test items or tasks, the number of items, and the ways students can respond. In this chapter, we also introduce the basic forms of selected-response and constructed-response item formats, with a focus on multiple-choice formats.

## Chapter Learning Objectives

1. Describe the purpose and key features of a test blueprint.
2. Summarize the advantages and disadvantages of selected-response items.
3. Recognize learning objectives that are more or less easily measured with selected-response items.
4. Identify and describe the differences between commonly used item formats.
5. Explain how multiple-choice items can be used to assess higher levels of cognitive tasks.

## A Blueprint Framework

The framework presented in this chapter can be used by instructors that are writing isolated items to be administered during the course of instruction, particularly through the use of a classroom response system. The framework also applies to short quizzes that might only contain four or five items. In any case, items should result from and be linked to learning objectives. When administered in the midst of a lecture or class activity, MC items can be designed to support understanding that facilitates instruction—instructional decisions can be made in terms of whether to proceed in a lesson, stop and review an important concept, or return to earlier concepts to build the additional scaffolding needed to support the learning of new material.

As an example of the context in this case, when the distractors (incorrect options) of the MC item are carefully constructed to contain common errors or misconceptions, knowing how many students retain those misconceptions can be powerful in informing instructional decisions. But this requires that the options be written to contain relevant misconceptions (one of the MC item-writing guidelines described in Chapter 4). In the case of using a classroom response system, you can quickly and meaningfully check student understanding and the presence of persistent misconceptions or problem-solving errors. But of course, this doesn't require a specific classroom response system.

## Why Is Validity So Important?

The purpose for testing drives our design decisions. First, we clearly state the purpose. For example: To assess student knowledge of the first major unit. Second, every unit has a set of learning objectives. For example: The students will be able to identify effectively constructed learning objectives. Third, that claim (as a result of the purpose) requires evidence (validation). To support that claim, we build the test in a way that supports the intended interpretation and use by design. An important source of evidence is the *Test Blueprint*. From the evidence, we can make inferences about our intended claims and meet the purpose of the test. Figure 3.1 illustrates these three components.

Other evidence that supports score interpretation and use has to do with test score quality, which is a function of item quality (i.e., following item-writing guidelines). We review these issues in Chapter 7. But first, we introduce the big ideas of test blueprints, with some guidance for constructing effective tests.

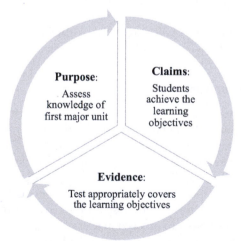

*Figure 3.1* The Connections Between Test Purpose, Claims, and Evidence

# What Is a Test Blueprint?

In testing at all levels, the Test Blueprint provides the Keys to the Kingdom—in other words, it provides essential validity evidence for test score interpretation and use. The test blueprint provides the design specifications (and is sometimes called test specifications). Just as in an architectural project, the blueprint lays out the design requirements—to achieve the desired result.

Consider the following straightforward argument:

1. I have learning objectives for Unit 1.
2. I need to test student achievement of the Unit 1 learning objectives.
3. I can write test items to test achievement of those learning objectives.
4. I adequately represent achievement in Unit 1 by balancing the number of items appropriately across those learning objectives.

That's all there is to it. We need to make sure that the unit is appropriately covered on the test so that the total score represents the unit in a way that supports our score interpretation. We've all taken tests that are unbalanced—tests in which half of the items are on a topic that was only briefly introduced or discussed or that was insignificant compared to other topics. Bottom line: The tests in a course should align with the course syllabus—the test should reflect what we, the instructors, say the course is about.

A great volume of research indicates that students learn while preparing for the test, while taking the test, and while reviewing the test (see the reviews by Black and Wiliam, 1998 and Phelps, 2012). Learning at all three stages is maximized when the test actually covers the core and important learning objectives—so the target of testing is clear and consistent with what actually happens in the course, which is hopefully consistent with the syllabus.

Another way to think about this is in the context of opportunity to learn (OTL) and instructional sensitivity. Tests provide the means to evaluate OTL and assume that students had the opportunity to learn the material. It is difficult to differentiate two competing interpretations of a test if we don't have evidence of OTL:

1. Scores reflect the extent to which students achieved the learning objectives.
2. Scores reflect the ability of the instructor to help students achieve the learning objectives.

This is why we need to clearly communicate the learning objectives, use them to organize our instructional activities and learning opportunities, and represent them appropriately on the test. We also need the test results to inform us about how students are doing on each learning objective in a way that can tell us what we need to reteach, provide additional opportunities for learning, or not to worry about and move on. Test scores can only do this if they represent the contents of instruction (are instructionally sensitive) and those things that students have had adequate opportunity to learn. We want to be able to say that because of our instruction, students are achieving the learning objectives—students who have had instruction do well on the items, whereas students who have not been instructed do poorly on the items.

In creating a test blueprint, we can specify a number of conditions to help us design an effective test:

1. How many items can be administered in the available time?—or—How many items do we need to administer to meet the purpose of the test?
2. What types of items can be used to test the relevant learning objectives?
3. What are the specific content areas given in the learning objectives? How should these be weighted to match the importance of the learning objectives?
4. What are the cognitive levels, tasks, or processes described in the learning objectives? How should these be weighted?

The answers to these questions have implications for validity—as they determine (or limit) the kinds of interpretations we can make of resulting scores.

> A test blueprint provides for greater equity in how we evaluate students, particularly across sections and years of a course.

When the test blueprint matches the learning objectives, instruction, and opportunities to learn, the resulting test is more likely to be a true reflection of the course and an appropriate tool to evaluate student performance. An equality approach would be to administer the exact same exam year after year—regardless of how topics roll out each year or how much time and emphasis we put on various topics each year or the extent to which new topics are introduced by us or our students. Using the same test may seem like the right way to evaluate students—equally—but fails to recognize that each year, there are likely to be different needs in terms of teaching and learning. Equity requires us to meet those unique needs and provides for fairer student evaluation.

### Creating a Test Blueprint

Each unit in a course has learning objectives (if not, return to Chapter 2). The learning objectives from each unit represented on the test need to be weighted in the test blueprint. But how do we determine the weights? Consider the following questions:

1. How much time was spent on each topic?
2. How important are the topics in the field?

3. What topics are worth learning and studying for?
4. What topics and skills are assessed in other ways (not via tests)?

Answers to these questions can help determine the proportion of the test devoted to each topic area—which then tells us how many items to write.

Consider a unit test that includes four content topic areas (A, B, C, and D) and three cognitive tasks (Remember, Understand, and Apply). We spent most of the unit time on the two most important topics (40% on A and 40% on B), with the remaining time and emphasis on two less important topics (10% on C and 10% on D). We also focused most attention to principles of application, so that we assign 20% to Remember, 30% to Understand, and 50% to Apply. This is represented in the illustration of the test blueprint that follows (Figure 3.2).

To end this example in a simple way, let's say we want to write a test with 100 items. We can now distribute the number of items to topics and cognitive tasks in a way that reflects our weights so that the content and skills tested provide us with the relevant evidence given the learning objectives of the unit. For example, if 40% of the items should cover topic A, then 40 items will be written to tap this topic. Among those 40 items, 50% should be application items, so we write 20 application items tapping topic A, and so on. However, not every content area may be associated with the same balance of cognitive tasks.

Consider the test blueprint for a course on educational measurement, covering the first third of the course. We've determined that 40 items can be administered in one course period (75 minutes—which approximates one item per two minutes). Six topic areas were covered in this part of the course (relatively evenly, ranging from 10% to 25% emphasis) with two cognitive tasks, including Remember (35%) and Understand/Apply (65%). The following blueprint distributes the 40 items according to the proportions across topics and cognitive tasks (Figure 3.3).

Notice that the number of items doesn't match exactly the percentages intended in each cell. For instance, the Reliability items are split equally (3 and 3) across the two cognitive tasks whereas there are more Validity items written for Understand/Apply (8 items or 80% of 10) than for Remember (2 items, or 20% of 10). This is because for Reliability, the course content emphasized

| Topic | Remember | Understand | Apply | Emphasis |
|---|---|---|---|---|
| A | 8 | 12 | 20 | 40% |
| B | 8 | 12 | 20 | 40% |
| C | 2 | 3 | 5 | 10% |
| D | 2 | 3 | 5 | 10% |
| Emphasis | 20% | 30% | 50% | 100% |

*Figure 3.2* Example Test Blueprint

| Content Topic | Cognitive Task | | Total | |
|---|---|---|---|---|
| | Remember | Understand/Apply | # | % |
| Classical Test Theory | 3 | 3 | 6 | 15% |
| Scores and Scales | 2 | 4 | 6 | 15% |
| Big Testing Concepts | 3 | 5 | 8 | 20% |
| Reliability | 3 | 3 | 6 | 15% |
| Validity | 2 | 8 | 10 | 25% |
| Basic Stats | 1 | 3 | 4 | 10% |
| Total # | 14 | 26 | 40 | |
| Total % | 35% | 65% | | 100% |

*Figure 3.3* Educational Measurement Course Test Blueprint

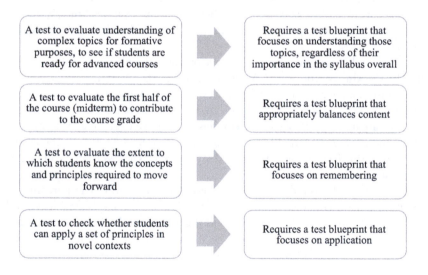

*Figure 3.4* Tests With Different Purposes Require Different Types of Blueprints

knowledge (learning terms and definitions) just as much as understanding and application (determining what kind of reliability applies to different test purposes, etc.). And for validity, the course emphasized understanding and application at a much higher level than simple knowledge (identifying the kinds of validity evidence relevant to different test score interpretations and uses, how to conduct validity studies, how contexts impact validity).

| Content | Remember | Understand | Apply | Analyze | Evaluate | # of items | % of test by content |
|---|---|---|---|---|---|---|---|
| Topic 1 | | | | | | | |
| Topic 2 | | | | | | | |
| Topic 3 | | | | | | | |
| . . . | | | | | | | |
| # of items | | | | | | | |
| % of test by cognitive level | | | | | | | |

*Figure 3.5* A Generic Test Blueprint Including Five Cognitive Tasks

Test blueprints provide a strong guide for item writing and test design, but as an instructor, you make the final determination of how to cover the content appropriately (see Figure 3.4). But remember the goals of grading described in Chapter 1. Tests designed for formative purposes (to check understanding or evaluate the adequacy of our instruction) should be weighted less—as we intend to use that information to improve teaching and learning. We want grades to reflect learning and achievement, and so we weight tests designed for summative purposes, those designed to contribute to grades, more heavily. Just as we want the interpretations about content mastery to be valid (through the appropriate design of test blueprints), we also want the interpretations about overall course achievement (through appropriately weighted grades) to be valid (see Figure 3.5).

## What Are the Most Common Test Item Formats?

Having developed the test blueprint, the next step is identifying appropriate item format(s). The available item formats have in common three basic components:

1. A question or task for the test taker,
2. some conditions or rules regarding the required response, and
3. scoring rules or procedures.

Furthermore, nearly all item formats can be classified in three groups based on the second and third components of response conditions and scoring procedures:

1. Selected response (SR) that is objectively scored,
2. constructed response that can be objectively scored (CROS), and
3. constructed response that is subjectively scored (CRSS).

This chapter focuses on SR items. Because of their unique nature and purposes, CROS and CRSS items are not discussed further here. The *Handbook of Test*

*Development* provides chapters that allow us to explore these more subjective assessment options (see Haladyna and Rodriguez, 2013; Lane and Iwatani, 2016; and Swygert and Williamson, 2016).

## What Are the Advantages and Disadvantages of SR Items?

There are multiple reasons for utilizing SR item formats for tests in college courses. As mentioned in the introduction and Chapter 1, SR items are efficient tools for collecting information about a broad range of KSAs, covering

*Table 3.1* Advantages and Disadvantages of SR Items

| Advantages | Disadvantages |
| --- | --- |
| • Allows for broad coverage of content. | • Challenging to construct high-quality items. |
| • Can be used to measure many different objectives (described in what follows). | • Time consuming to construct well. |
| • Can provide diagnostic information about errors in thinking, misconceptions, etc. | • Not good for measuring innovative thinking, creating something. |
| • Easy to score; can be machine scored. | • Students are familiar with the format. |
| • Efficient for large classes. | • May be affected by student reading skills. |
| • Able to control difficulty to some degree. | • May encourage overtesting recall. |
| | • Doesn't reflect real-world problem solving. |

*Table 3.2* Example Learning Objectives That Can Be Measured Well or Not So Well by SR Items

| Measured well | Not measured as well |
| --- | --- |
| • Analyzing conditions and phenomena | • Explaining reasoning or thinking |
| • Applying concepts and principles in new contexts | • Providing information to support an argument |
| • Evaluating cause-and-effect associations | • Organizing thoughts |
| • Evaluating the relevance of information or evidence | • Performing tasks |
| • Solving problems | • Producing innovative ideas |
| • Discriminating between facts and opinions | • Providing examples |
| • Interpreting graphical displays | |
| • Drawing inferences from data | |

lots of content in a short period of time, and they are easy to administer and score (see Figure 3.1). Because we can construct items to provide information about common misconceptions, misinformation, and problem-solving errors (see the section on distractor development in the next chapter), they can also provide diagnostic information. Table 3.2 provides example learning objectives well suited for SR items.

## What Are the Most Common SR Formats?

We review common SR item formats here. For a complete review of the many SR formats and additional examples, see Haladyna and Rodriguez (2013). The formats reviewed here include:

1.  multiple choice
2.  multiple response
3.  complex type-K
4.  context-based item sets
5.  true-false, multiple true-false
6.  matching

Each format is described and presented with an example.

### Multiple Choice (MC)

As the most common item format in achievement tests, this format is the focus of the book, and Chapter 4 is devoted to item-writing guidelines and other considerations for MC items. An MC item includes a question with options or a statement where the options complete the sentence.

> If a distribution of test scores is negatively skewed, standardizing the scores into z-scores will result in what type of distribution?
>
> A.  Positively skewed
> B.  Normal
> C.  Negatively skewed

### Multiple-Response MC

The multiple-response MC item is an MC item with the potential of multiple correct options, typically where all correct options must be selected to get credit for the item. This format is gaining use in some standardized testing programs (e.g., GRE). There is little research in the literature on its quality. For classroom tests, it is very important for students to know that it may be possible to select multiple correct answers, but realize that an instruction to select "the best answer" will not work with this format. Some recommend partial-credit scoring if one or some of the correct options are selected but not all of them. For these reasons, we recommend against using multiple-response MC items and recommend considering multiple true-false items instead (described below).

Which interpretations are criterion referenced?

    A.   Eighty percent of the class scored above a *T*-score of 55.
    B.   Hattie scored above the 95th percentile requirement to win the scholarship.
    C.   Jean Luc answered 80 percent of the items correctly.
    D.   Mariana scored in the Exceeds Standards range on the reading test.
    E.   Santiago's score is three standard deviations above the state mean.

### Complex Type-K MC

The complex MC format is often called the type-K item. It includes a standard MC item, where there are multiple correct responses and the options selected by students include different combinations of the responses. This item format is common in the health sciences. Many times, there are multiple conditions, symptoms, clinical tests, or possible treatments that are appropriate. For these reasons, it is important for students to distinguish among sets of options that provide the best answer.

Research has shown that complex MC items are more difficult and require more reading time. It may be possible to answer these questions correctly with partial knowledge, when one option is known as absolutely correct or incorrect, allowing the student to eliminate certain option combinations. Research has also found that this format tends to reduce item discrimination, the ability of the item to distinguish between higher-ability and lower-ability students—which is an important indicator of item quality. This also leads to lower test score reliability.

Which scores are developmental norm-referenced scores?

    1.   Normal curve equivalents
    2.   Grade equivalent
    3.   Mental age
    4.   Percentiles

        A.   1 and 2
        B.   1 and 4
        C.   2 and 3
        D.   2 and 4

### Context-Based Item Sets

Context-based item sets can be composed of items in any format, but what makes this format different is that the item set is associated with context material. Providing context materials, such as a reading passage, graphic, picture, data table, or any course-related material, is a great way to create more authentic assessment and test higher-order thinking skills. A test can provide authentic scenarios through which we can test students' KSAs. This also helps test higher-order thinking skills, as it is easier to test application, analysis, and evaluation skills by presenting a real-life context or a scenario on which to base the test items.

Consider the following example, where a test blueprint can provide the context for several questions:

*Blueprint for Midterm Statistics Exam*

| Content Areas | Cognitive Task | | | Total |
|---|---|---|---|---|
| | *Remembering* | *Understanding* | *Applying* | |
| Frequency Distributions | # | # | # | 20% |
| Transformations | # | # | # | 10% |
| Central Tendency | # | # | # | 30% |
| Variability | # | # | # | 40% |
| Total | 20% | 30% | 50% | 100% |

From the test blueprint, what appears to be the **most** important topic covered?

    A.   Frequency Distributions
    B.   Transformations
    C.   Central Tendency
    <u>D.</u>   Variability

If the statistics exam will have 50 items, how many *Frequency Distributions* items should be written that require the cognitive task of *Applying*?

    <u>A.</u>   5
    B.   10
    C.   15
    D.   25

### True-False, Multiple True-False

You can ask many more true-false (TF) items than MC items in the same time period, covering a lot of content in a short time period. TF items are also very easy to score (objectively). However, there are numerous reasons to avoid using them. It is very hard to write TF items that are unambiguously true or false. TF items tend to measure low levels of cognitive processes, typically remembering, with a 50% chance of guessing correctly.

Indicate whether each statement is True (T) or False (F) by circling T or F.

The vectors $\underline{a}' = (10, 12, 9)$ and $\underline{a} = \begin{bmatrix} 10 \\ 12 \\ 9 \end{bmatrix}$ are equal          T / F

$\underline{a} + (\underline{b} + \underline{c}) = \underline{a} + \underline{b} + \underline{c}$                    T / F

$\underline{a}' \underline{b} = \underline{a} \underline{b}'$                                                T / F

There is limited diagnostic information available in responses to TF items, limiting their use for formative purposes. However, in multiple TF items, diagnostic information can be obtained, similarly to MC items.

These statements accurately reflect ideas about reliability.

|  | True | False |
|---|---|---|
| a. Some kinds of test errors are more important than others. | ☒ | ☐ |
| b. Some of the variance of test scores may be attributed to characteristics of the test takers. | ☒ | ☐ |
| c. Test reliability is consistent, every time a test is used. | ☐ | ☒ |
| d. The true score plus the error score equals the observed test score. | ☒ | ☐ |

TF items can also be written as either/or items, where the response options are one thing or the other. Consider the following example. It could have been written to suggest each statistic is an index of item difficulty, true or false, but since the statistics are of one type or the other, this format is more direct and better.

Do these statistics provide information about item difficulty or item discrimination?

|  |  | Difficulty | Discrimination |
|---|---|---|---|
| a. | proportion correct | ☒ | ☐ |
| b. | a-parameter | ☐ | ☒ |
| c. | b-parameter | ☒ | ☐ |
| d. | p-value | ☒ | ☐ |
| e. | point-biserial | ☐ | ☒ |

Guidelines for writing true-false items:

1. Statements should be based on important content, not trivial content.
2. Statements should clearly express a single idea in a declarative sentence.
3. Statements should be unequivocally true or false, with no exceptions.
4. Do not use statements taken directly from textbooks or course materials.
5. Do not write negative statements.
6. Write both versions of each statement, a true and a false version. Of course, select only one version for the test.
7. Avoid specific determiners such as *always*, *never*, *all*, *none*, and the like.

In addition, most of the guidelines for MC item writing also apply to writing TF items. MC item-writing guidelines are described in Chapter 4.

## Matching

Matching items do not require a high reading ability and can cover a lot of content in a short period of time, providing many of the benefits of TF items. However, it is challenging to create matching items that require more than simple recall or remembering. It is possible to create a set of conditions with plausible outcomes or implications, requiring the application of criteria or analysis of causes and effects or other higher-level thinking skills.

Directions: On the line next to each study method, place the letter of the type of validity evidence that is most likely obtained from the method. Choices of validity evidence may be used once, more than once, or not at all.

| Validity Study Methods | Validity Evidence |
| --- | --- |
| _B_ Correlations with future performance | A. Concurrent criterion related |
| _A_ Correlations with current grades | B. Predictive criterion related |
| _E_ Correlations among subscores | C. Content related |
| _E_ Confirmatory factor analysis | D. Response processes |
| _D_ Think-alouds | E. Internal structure |
| _C_ Alignment to professional standards | |

Guidelines for writing matching items:

1. Each stimulus and response option should be homogenous (of the same content and type).
2. Instructions should clearly state the basis for matching and that responses can be used more than once or not at all.
3. Write no more than 10 stimuli, keeping each brief with short phrases or single words.

4.  Include more responses or stimuli to prevent identifying the correct response through elimination.

Because we focus on MC items in the remaining chapters, here is an example of a poorly constructed matching item set. Can you identify the item-writing flaws?

> Directions: The descriptions on the left can be attributed to one of the important individuals or key terms on the right. Match the descriptions with one individual or key term. Each individual or key term may be used once, more than once, or not at all.

| Description | Individuals & Key Terms |
| --- | --- |
| _f_ Explored applications of latent trait theory to testing | a. H. Mann |
| _e_ The summarized the principles of true score theory | b. C.C. Brigham and R.M. Yerkes |
| _c_ Offered the first course in educational measurement | c. E.L. Thorndike |
| _a_ He advocated for written examinations in education | d. Multiple-Choice Items |
| _d_ Referred to as the "new-type" tests in the 1920s | e. H. Gulliksen |
| _j_ Introduced the term "mental tests" | f. F.M. Lord |
| _h_ He tested people to promote segregation | g. L.L. Thurstone |
| _g_ The author of *The Reliability and Validity of Tests* | h. H.H. Goddard |
| _i_ Studied the existence of general intelligence | i. C. Spearman |
| _b_ He promoted the development of eugenics | j. J.M. Cattell |
| _k_ An attribute that is not directly observable | k. Latent Trait |
| _l_ A quantitative method | l. Measurement |

There are a number of item-writing flaws:

1.  There should be a different number of Descriptions and Individuals/Key Terms. A student could identify the final response through elimination.
2.  The set of statements should be homogenous, so only include descriptions of individuals or descriptions of key terms. These should be in two different matching sets.

3. The Individuals for option b include two people, but the Description starts with "He promoted . . . ." This suggests one person, but the answer is two people.
4. The last two Descriptions are based on the two Key Terms on the right, and they are in the same order in both lists.
5. There are 12 descriptive statements; too many.
6. Descriptive statement *e* is also grammatically incorrect; it should begin "He proposed . . ."
7. Some Description statements are phrases, whereas others are complete sentences. They should be homogenous in structure.

## How Do We Write MC Items to Tap Higher-Order Thinking?

MC items have a bad reputation for only measuring recall—remembering. But we can write items that tap higher-order cognitive skills, including understanding, applying, analyzing, and evaluating. It seems like a real stretch to measure creating skills with MC items, but we wouldn't say it's impossible. To increase the cognitive skills assessed in your MC items, consider the following recommendations. Many of these come from Tom Haladyna (1997), who has dedicated much of his career to improving the skills of item writers.

1. Use novel situations, contexts, conditions, scenarios, graphical displays, and other materials. But make sure students have had experience with the kinds of materials used in the test.
2. Real-world contexts provide practical and engaging problems and allow us to test students' abilities to generalize KSAs.
3. Build in a requirement for reasoning in the item. Often this can be done by extending instructional content so that students must transfer their knowledge and understanding in broader ways.
4. Require students to correctly interpret the problem.
5. Ask students to hypothesize or predict outcomes, given sets of conditions.
6. Require students to determine the principles or components that are relevant.
7. Ask students to select reasons or justifications for a result presented in the item, scenario, or data display.
8. Ask students to select a course of action, given the problem or conditions.
9. Present a scenario with specific circumstances so that students can select the most likely outcome or result.
10. Create a scenario that is not complete, where students identify the missing pieces.
11. Given relevant criteria, ask students to select solutions to various problems.

## MC Items With Justification

Arthur Odom (1995) created a measure to diagnose student misconceptions in biology regarding diffusion and osmosis. He argued that such measures allow instructors to develop lessons that change conceptual understanding. He began by defining misconceptions as student ideas that are "different from those generally accepted by scientists" (p. 409). He created a list of 22 propositional knowledge statements required for understanding diffusion and osmosis. Two example items include (p. 414):

1a.  Suppose there is a large beaker full of clear water and a drop of blue dye is added to the beaker of water. Eventually the water will turn a light blue color. The process responsible for blue dye becoming evenly distributed through the water is:
   a.   Osmosis
   b.   Diffusion
   c.   A reaction between water and dye

1b.  The reason for my answer is:
   a.   The lack of a membrane means that osmosis and diffusion cannot occur.
   b.   There is movement of particles between regions of different concentrations.
   c.   The dye separates into small particles and mixes with water.
   d.   The water moves from one region to another.

Any other combination of responses other than b (for 1a.) an b (for 1b.) comprise different forms of misconceptions. A more recent version of the Diffusion and Osmosis Diagnostic Test has been developed and studied (Fisher, Williams, and Lineback, 2011).

### Item Starters

While Ron Berk (1996) was a professor at the Johns Hopkins University School of Nursing, he created a guide to MC item formats that measure complex cognitive outcomes. In this, he provided an excellent set of item "starters" that can be used as models to write test items. Here are the generic stems that Berk recommended:

### Prediction

1.  If . . ., then what happens?
2.  What will probably happen?
3.  What would happen if . . .?
4.  What is the cause of . . .?

**Evaluation and Decision Making**

1.  Which is the most or least important, significant . . .?
2.  Which of . . . is the most or least effective . . .?
3.  Which action, decision, procedure . . . demonstrates/illustrates . . .?
4.  What is the most/least appropriate action/response . . .?
5.  What is the best/worst step/procedure . . .?
6.  What is the most useful/useless strategy/approach . . .?
7.  What is the best/worst action/decision/advice . . .?

Berk also offered a number of generic stems for measuring complex cognitive outcomes. These examples are slightly modified from his suggestions:

1.  What is the effect of . . .?
2.  What principle explains . . .?
3.  Which exemplifies the principle . . .?
4.  Which procedure should be used when . . .?
5.  Which generalization can be made from the data . . .?
6.  Which feature is a major strength/weakness of . . .?
7.  Which approach will result in . . .?
8.  This situation will create . . .?
9.  Which consequence will (likely) result from . . .?
10. What is the most effective/efficient/complicated solution to . . .?
11. This scenario is an example of the principle . . .?
12. What is the first step following . . .?
13. What is the next step after . . .?
14. What is the (most) appropriate action to resolve . . .?

Recognize that we could change the key terms in each stem by relying on a thesaurus. For example, using the Microsoft Word thesaurus (while writing this sentence), there are several synonyms for the word "effect," including "result," "consequence," "outcome," "conclusion," "influence." This is a good way to find words so that we can ask several questions that vary on a common theme, and not be repetitive. Keeping students' interest level high is a way to engage them in the test and encourage more accurate responses.

## How Do We Put Items Together in a Test?

Hopefully, you didn't just sit down one night and write all of your test questions. Also, hopefully you are not just using last year's test without reviewing the content in light of the course experiences from the current year. It's best to write items as the course progresses. Many items can be written throughout a unit or section of the course. Lectures and class discussions provide a great deal of fuel for test items. Keep notes with important topics, contexts, problems, questions, and issues raised by students from each session. Test items can be effective when they address the questions, challenges, and issues brought up through lectures and class discussions.

Here are just a few guidelines for putting everything together in a test form.

1.   Give clear and explicit directions (don't assume anything).
2.   Make sure the items are consistent with the test blueprint.
3.   Arrange items based on test content (with similar content together).
4.   Leave enough room for complete answers to constructed-response items.
5.   Do not split questions across a page—or reading or graphic materials associated with an item, if possible.

### Provide Clear Instruction

Instructions for the test should state how many items in each format are on the test and how many points each item format is worth. For each section of the test, you can state how much time students should spend on the section given the number of items and their format. Also, provide some instruction about the possibility of guessing—don't encourage it, but students should answer all questions. All of this is to help students be more efficient in their effort. An example general instruction to a test is:

> This exam consists of 25 multiple-choice items each worth one point, 5 constructed-response items each worth two points, and two context-dependent item sets, one with 5 questions worth 5 points and one with 5 questions worth 10 points; 50 points in total. Your score on this exam will be the number of MC items you have marked correctly and the number of points you obtain on the constructed-response items. Select the best answer to each item, but do not spend too much time on any one item. The exam is designed to be completed within 1 hour, but you have 75 minutes. If an item is unclear, feel free to write a comment directly on the test form for reference when we review the test. This exam is provided as a tool to measure achievement of the course objectives for the units covered to date.

### Consider the Amount of Time Available for Taking the Test

It is difficult to estimate the amount of time it takes to respond to a single MC item. If the item requires remembering or understanding and the test takers are native speakers of the language of the test, 30 to 60 seconds per item should be sufficient. If the items require more thought or higher-order thinking, 1½ minutes per item should be sufficient. If the test takers are not native speakers of the language of the test and if the items require more consideration of graphic materials, reading passages, or computation (or estimation), it may take as much as 2 minutes per item. Some items will only take 15 to 30 seconds, whereas others will take 2 minutes of consideration and reconsideration. For typical college courses, 45 MC items can be administered in 60 minutes—and of course, for items requiring more extensive reading, graph analysis, computation, or estimation, more time will be needed.

### Ask a Colleague to Review the Test

Tests used to contribute toward grades in a big way should be reviewed by a colleague. Colleagues are in a good position to notice problems with test items, including things such as having no correct answer or multiple correct answers, confusing terms, clues to the correct answer, and unnecessarily complex language and maybe even provide advice about content that is irrelevant or potentially misleading. Colleagues can also provide guidance as to whether the problem or issue presented in the test item is worth asking or if it is trivial and not important.

The department could develop a culture of assessment, supporting instructors' abilities to develop meaningful, appropriate, and useful learning objectives and assessment practices that allow for meaningful, appropriate, and useful evaluation of those learning objectives. An important part of a culture of assessment is the shared responsibility and collegiality among instructors. This includes the practice of reviewing each other's assessment activities and tests. Not only are we supporting each other in our important roles as instructors, but we are learning from each other as well.

In large-scale standardized testing, item writing is a collaborative effort. Subject-matter experts (like you) are trained to develop items tapping relevant content and cognitive tasks. The items are reviewed by lead item writers and sometimes returned to item writers for editing. Test items are also reviewed by sensitivity specialists or committees, where members look for potential bias due to content-irrelevant features, including gender, race/ethnicity, region, and language. Items are piloted or field tested in a way that allows us to gather student responses to the items without having the item count in the score. These data are used to evaluate the quality of the item and the extent to which each item contributes to the total score. They also provide for a means to do more technical analyses of possible item bias (differential item functioning examines the extent to which items function differently in various groups). The item might then undergo additional review for possible bias.

> There is no way we can achieve the same level of item development in classroom testing as we see in standardized testing. But this does not mean the quality of our items is limited.

It is difficult to improve our item quality without some preparation or training in item writing. Oftentimes, we (the college instructors) are the only ones writing and reviewing items for our tests. If we follow the item-writing guidelines presented here (which include the recommendations of many other experts), we can reduce the potential errors or mistakes in item writing, especially the most common errors instructors make in developing test items. There are some things we can do to evaluate the quality of our test items, and these are discussed in Chapter 7. But let's keep the focus on two very important points:

1.    High-quality test items provide important evidence of the quality of teaching and learning to support teaching and learning.
2.    Tests typically contribute to course grades, which are indicators of student achievement and their knowledge, skills, and abilities.

Grades are high stakes. We often talk about classroom assessment as low stakes (compared to high-stakes graduation tests, college admissions tests, or certification and licensure tests). But for many of our students, grades are high stakes, as they often provide information for decision making—*Am I in the right major?*—or provide access to future opportunities—*Is this student able to succeed in a graduate degree program?*

## Applications

This chapter defines and presents examples of test blueprints and shows how a blueprint establishes content validity evidence for a test. Commonly used SR item formats are described with examples, and recommendations for writing, revising, and administering these item formats are provided, along with recommendations for writing SR items to assess higher levels of cognitive tasks. In the following applications, you will create your own test blueprint and evaluate the appropriateness of the item formats, content, and cognitive tasks outlined within your blueprint.

1.    Create a test blueprint showing the distribution of items over cognitive tasks and content areas within a course test. Your blueprint should represent important content, according to the learning objectives you developed in Chapter 2, and should utilize cognitive tasks that are appropriate to each content area.
2.    Write a matching item for chapter learning objective 4: Identify and describe the differences between commonly used item formats. The choices could involve matching the name of the item format with a certain feature, strength, or limitation of that format.
3.    Go through the items in a course test to determine whether each item format is justified and appropriately used. Convert multiple-response MC and complex MC items to other formats such as MC or multiple true-false items.
4.    Evaluate the cognitive tasks assessed within your own test items. Are these tasks appropriate for the content covered? How can the items be modified to improve the cognitive tasks assessed?

# References

Berk, R. A. (1996). A consumer's guide to multiple-choice item formats that measure complex cognitive outcomes. In National Evaluation Systems (Eds.), *From policy to practice: Proceedings from the Teacher Certification Testing Conference* (pp. 101–127). Amherst, MA: Author. Retrieved at www.pearsonassessments.com/teacherlicensure/conference-on-teaching/publications/from-policy-to-practice.html

Black, P., and Wiliam, D. (1998). Assessment and classroom learning. *Assessment in Education, 5*, 7–74.

Fisher, K. M., Williams, K. S., and Lineback, J. E. (2011). Osmosis and diffusion conceptual assessment. *CBE Life Science Education, 10*(4), 418–429.

Haladyna, T. M. (1997). *Writing test items to evaluate higher order thinking.* Needham Heights, MA: Allyn & Bacon.

Haladyna, T. M., and Rodriguez, M. C. (2013). *Developing and validating test items.* New York, NY: Routledge.

Lane, S., and Iwatani, E. (2016). Design of performance assessments in education. In S. Lane, M. R. Raymond, and T. M. Haladyna (Eds.), *Handbook of test development* (2nd ed., pp. 274–293). New York, NY: Routledge.

Odom, A. L. (1995). Secondary & college biology students' misconceptions about diffusion & osmosis. *The American Biology Teacher, 57*(7), 409–415. Available in a prepublication version (1993) at www.mlrg.org/proc3pdfs/Odom_DiffusionOsmosis.pdf

Phelps, R. P. (2012). The effect of testing on student achievement, 1910–2010. *International Journal of Testing, 12*, 21–43.

Swygert, K. A., and Williamson, D. M. (2016). Using performance tasks in credentialing tests. In S. Lane, M. R. Raymond, and T. M. Haladyna (Eds.), *Handbook of test development* (2nd ed., pp. 294–312). New York, NY: Routledge.

# 4 Writing Multiple-Choice Items

In this chapter, we present a list of guidelines for writing MC items and demonstrate their application with examples. After some background on the development of the guidelines, we provide recommendations on the selection of item content. We then review the basic structure of the MC item and present the item-writing guidelines in detail.

## Chapter Learning Objectives

1. Describe the development of an MC item, including the basic structure and strategies for selecting item content.
2. Explain, with examples, how common misunderstandings of students can be used to improve MC options.
3. Identify in existing MC items violations of the guidelines and provide suggestions for revision.
4. Utilize the guidelines to write effective MC items in your subject-matter area.
5. Explain the most important considerations when targeting a certain level of item difficulty.

## Background on the Guidelines

Item writers now have a strong set of item-writing guidelines that support item development and validation (see Haladyna and Rodriguez, 2013). Although these guidelines have mostly been evaluated in the context of K–12 classrooms, there is some evidence to support their use in college classrooms. Moreover, many of these guidelines are commonly found in the item-writing training materials of large-scale testing programs, for example in guidelines for K–12 state testing programs; many college, graduate, and professional school admissions testing programs; as well as certificate and licensure testing programs.

Measurement specialists and researchers have accumulated evidence of the effectiveness of professional development opportunities to improve item-writing skills of college instructors. We know that college instructors can improve their item-writing and test-development skills. With some training, instructors can write items that are more cognitively challenging, with better-functioning distractors and fewer item-writing flaws (Abdulghani et al., 2015; Naeem, van der Vleuten, and Alfaris, 2012). Some researchers have focused on the use of MC items in the health sciences, including medicine (Downing, 2005; Jozefowicz et al., 2002) and nursing (Tarrant, Knierim, Hayes, and Ware, 2006; Tarrant and Ware, 2008), illustrating how common and problematic item-writing flaws can be. Some of these flaws tend to be about the stem or question, including unfocused stems, negatively worded or contradictory stems, or stems with unnecessary information. Most flaws tend to be about the options, including no correct or multiple correct answers, implausible distractors, more details in the correct answer, or options with clues. These are addressed below.

The MC item-writing guidelines address the four aspects of item content, the structural format of the item, the stem, and the options. Each guideline is presented in a systematic manner, starting with a statement of the guideline, details on why it is important (evidence based when possible), and an example item that violates the guideline followed by an improved version of the item.

## How Do We Identify and Select Test Item Content?

Your instructional learning objectives provide the first level of support for identifying the appropriate content for test items. Beyond this, if you use a textbook, many textbooks now have learning objectives at the beginning of each chapter, which attempt to identify key learning targets. However, these may not align with the instructional approach you take in your course, so published objectives should be reviewed carefully in light of your own intentions.

Good resources for test item content are class lectures, discussions, and activities. Following each session, keep a list of main ideas, concepts, and issues discussed. Take particular note of the challenges students faced or misconceptions they may have offered in discussions or questions. Often, questions raised by students can be rephrased to become excellent test items. When you collect these ideas for test items, it is often helpful to write them in declarative complete sentences. This makes the content available for a number of item formats (reviewed earlier).

Another source of test items is the item bank that accompanies your textbook if you are using a textbook. However, these items are typically quickly written, often by undergraduate or graduate students. They have not necessarily been piloted or reviewed by measurement specialists and almost never come with quality information—no evidence of their statistical quality. In our review of textbook item banks, many are poorly written and contain multiple item-writing flaws.

Because of this, we used item banks from many different college course textbooks to provide examples of poor and better test items in the next chapter. And, to be sure, we are not content experts in every possible field, so we may have missed technical flaws in many of these items, as the question itself or the options may be technically inadequate, inappropriate, or simply wrong. It's nearly impossible to know if an item has only one best answer, no best answer, or multiple best answers unless you are a subject-matter expert. It is your subject-matter expertise that makes you qualified to judge the content adequacy of a test item. So if you use a textbook item bank as a resource, be sure to review the item using the item-writing guidelines we provide here. And feel free to edit, modify, or alter the item to meet your instructional learning objectives.

## What Is the Structure of an MC Item?

Stem = the question or phrase requiring a response
Options = the possible responses, including the key and distractors
Key = correct option
Distractor = incorrect option

*Example:*

What will improve test score reliability? [STEM]

A.  Asking questions on many different topics [DISTRACTOR]
B.  Increasing the number of items [KEY]
C.  Sampling high-ability students [DISTRACTOR]        } OPTIONS
D.  Using five or more options [DISTRACTOR]

## Item-Writing Guidelines

These guidelines are primarily based on the work of Haladyna and Rodriguez (2013), reflecting decades of item-writing research and guidance. In addition, we reviewed dozens of guidelines from offices of teaching and learning at a variety of colleges and universities to secure the most comprehensive guidance available. Some of these guidelines have a research basis. The empirical evidence for these guidelines is comprehensively reviewed by Haladyna, Downing, and Rodriguez (2003) and Haladyna and Rodriguez (2013). We simply state when an item is research based in the introduction to the guideline.

Each guideline is described here, including examples of MC items with poor and better versions. In Chapter 6, we provide many examples of items from different fields, again including poor and better versions.

## Content Concerns

1. Base each item on one aspect of content and one cognitive task.
2. Use new material and context to elicit higher-order cognitive skills.
3. Keep the content of items independent of one another.
4. Test important content. Avoid overly specific and overly general content.
5. Avoid opinions and trick items.

## Formatting and Style Concerns

6. Format each item vertically instead of horizontally.
7. Edit and proof items.
8. Keep the language complexity of items at an appropriate level for the class being tested.
9. Minimize the amount of reading in each item. Avoid window dressing.

## Writing the Stem

10. Write the stem as a complete question or a phrase to be completed by the options.
11. State the main idea in the stem clearly and concisely and not in the options.
12. Word the stem positively; avoid negative phrasing.
13. Move into the stem any words that are repeated in each option.

## Writing the Options

14. Write as many options as are needed, given the topic and cognitive task; three options are usually sufficient.
15. Make all distractors plausible.
16. Make sure that only one option is the correct answer.
17. Place options in logical or numerical order.
18. Vary the location of the right answer evenly across the options.
19. Keep options independent; options should not overlap.
20. Avoid using the options *none of the above, all of the above,* and *I don't know.*
21. Word the options positively; avoid negative words such as "not."
22. Avoid giving clues to the right answer:
    a. Keep the length of options about equal.
    b. Avoid specific determiners including "always," "never," "completely," and "absolutely."
    c. Avoid clang associations, options identical to or resembling words in the stem.
    d. Avoid pairs or triplets of options that clue the test taker to the correct choice.
    e. Avoid blatantly absurd, ridiculous, or humorous options.
    f. Keep options homogeneous in content and grammatical structure.

*Content Concerns*

**1.  Base each item on one aspect of content and cognitive task.**

The main goal here is to make each item as direct and precise as possible—clearly stating the question, challenge, or problem being posed to the student. Many classroom test items are flawed because of failure to understand and follow this guideline.

Poor:    A very high positive correlation between academic aptitude and achievement is estimated with a random sample of college students, but we should expect a _____ correlation among a random sample of _____ students.

        A.   negative—high school
        B.   lower—honors
        C.   zero—first-year
        D.   higher—a larger sample of

The poor version is a common format, but it is asking for two different elements of content. In addition, option C is not plausible, as "zero" is too absolute. This item is less problematic than most, since both pieces of information are unique in each option. Consider this version:

Poor:    A very high positive correlation between academic aptitude and achievement is estimated with a random sample of college students, but we should expect a _____ correlation among a random sample of _____ students.

        A.   lower—high school
        B.   lower—honors
        C.   higher—high school
        D.   higher—honors

In both cases, we can improve measurement by focusing on one aspect of the task and then be more certain about the nature of student understanding or misunderstanding.

Better:    A correlation between academic aptitude and achievement is estimated from a random sample of college students. How will a second correlation from a random sample of honor students compare? The second correlation will be

        A.   lower.
        B.   similar.
        C.   higher.

Sometimes the complexity is subtle. The following question provides a question with two different scenarios when only one is required.

Poor:      What is the most likely shape of a distribution if it is unimodal, but the mean is different than the median or the median is different than the mode?

    A.   normal
    <u>B.</u>   skewed
    C.   leptokurtic

Better:    What is the most likely shape of a distribution if it is unimodal, but the mean is different than the mode?

    A.   normal
    <u>B.</u>   skewed
    C.   leptokurtic

**2.   Use new material and contexts to elicit higher-order cognitive skills.**

Avoid using direct quotes, examples, and other materials from textbooks, reading assignments, and lectures from class. This invites simple recall and remembering the materials. Novel material and contexts let you tap cognitive tasks that are more important and that measure the ability of students to generalize their knowledge and skills. The poor example that follows is based on the correlation item from guideline 1. With the context now removed, we're assessing recall of information rather than application to a new situation.

Poor:      A correlation is estimated using a heterogeneous sample of people. How will a second correlation from a more homogenous sample compare? The second correlation will be

    <u>A.</u>   lower.
    B.   similar.
    C.   higher.

At the end of this chapter, we provide a list of recommendations and question templates that can be used to measure higher-order thinking.

**3.   Keep the content of items independent of one another.**

This concern is more common with constructed-response items, particularly in mathematics, where the solution from one question is used to solve the next question. But this is also important in MC items.

The correct response to one item should not depend on the response to another item. If the student gets the first item incorrect, and the next item depends on this response, the next item will likely be answered incorrectly as well. You want each item to provide unique and independent information about a student's KSAs.

Poor:    If the mean is 50, the median is 40, and the mode is 30, what is the shape of the distribution?

    <u>A</u>.    positively skewed
    B.    normal
    C.    negatively skewed
    D.    unknown

Based on this distribution (from previous question), is the distribution symmetric?

    <u>A</u>.    No
    B.    Yes

Another way this can create problems is by providing clues to the correct answer. If the following question accompanied the first poor question, it might help the student realize the correct option to the preceding item.

A distribution that is positively skewed has one tail "pulled" or extended in which direction?

    A.    left
    <u>B</u>.    right

It is best to create unique and independent items. Many times, multiple items must be written that tap important content, but they should not be connected in any way.

**4.    Test important content. Avoid overly specific and overly general content.**

This guideline should really state: Test your course and instructional learning objectives. And those learning objectives should declare the important elements of knowledge, skills, and abilities that result from taking the class. There are many possible examples of overly specific questions that students should not be required to memorize.

Consider the following question from a course on educational and psychological measurement, which focuses on application of the principles of measurement.

Poor:    The reliability of the Hypochondria scale of the MMPI-2 is

    A.    .77.
    B.    .78.
    C.    .79.

There is no real answer to this question (it is hypothetical). Anyway, we should all cry being faced with such a question. But we can reclaim it.

Better:   Consider the following test question:

The reliability of the Hypochondria scale of the MMPI-2 is

A.  .77.
B.  .78.
C.  .79.

The item-writing flaw in this item is that it

A.  tests multiple cognitive tasks.
B.  is a trick item.
C.  includes overly specific content.

A better option might be to offer a series of MC items, each with an item-writing flaw, with a list of guidelines. The students can then match or identify the guideline being violated in each MC item.

Sometimes the content is simply too general. Not only do these tend to be easy items, we lose the opportunity to test content that is more important—content we want students to understand and be able to apply, analyze, and so on.

Poor:     Validity is important for

A.  test taker experience.
B.  test score interpretation.
C.  test-retest reliability.

Better:   Dropping poor items from a test on the basis of item analysis data alone will likely lower

A.  content-related validity.
B.  score reliability.
C.  average item difficulty.

The poor question is very general and doesn't really tap specific knowledge or understanding about validity—hopefully we all know now that we validate test score interpretations and uses. It is much more important to inquire about students' understanding of the characteristics and principles of validity and what affects it.

## 5.  Avoid opinions and trick items.

Opinion items often don't have a clear and consistent best option, as it depends on who you ask—someone's opinion. However, if the point is to connect the opinion with a specific person, then the item must include the source of the opinion. This is one of the dangers of true-false items; they are often written so that they appear to be opinions.

Poor:    School accountability testing should only be reported at the level of

   A.   students.
   B.   teachers.
   <u>C</u>.   schools.
   D.   school districts.

Better:   According to Professor Rodriguez, school accountability test results should be reported at the level of

   A.   students.
   B.   teachers.
   <u>C</u>.   schools.

This item still has a problem since the word "school" appears in both the stem and the options (clang association). If the term "school" is not used in the stem, then the level of accountability is left ambiguous, and any option could be correct. Unfortunately, it is sometimes not easy (or even possible) to ask questions we want without providing some level of clue to students.

Trick items are a different story. There is very little research on the use of trick items, but it is a common complaint from students. Dennis Roberts (1993) surveyed 174 college students and 41 college faculty, asking them to define trick questions. Nearly half reported that MC items can be trick items, with fewer reporting that true-false (20%), short-answer (3%), matching (1%), essay (1%), or any item format (27%) could be tricky. Most participants also reported that when trick questions appear on the test, it is deliberate. There were several themes that emerged from the definitions of trick items from these college students and faculty:

- The test developer intends to confuse or mislead the student.
- The content is trivial and not important.
- The content is at a level of precision not discussed in class—options are too similar to each other.
- The stem contains extra irrelevant information.
- There are multiple correct answers.
- The item measures knowledge that is presented in the opposite way from which it was presented in class.
- The item is so ambiguous, even the most knowledgeable student has to guess.

Roberts then created a 25-item test, with 13 of the items being trick items that included many of the issues presented in the tricky-item-characteristic list above (had irrelevant content, ambiguous stems, principles presented in the opposite way it was introduced in class, and others). More than 100 students were asked not to answer the items but simply to rate them in terms of the extent to which it may be a trick item on a 1 (not a trick item) to 4 (definitely a trick item) rating scale. Students were not effective at distinguishing between trick items and not-trick items. However, among the not-trick items, students were more accurate in their identification of the items (that they actually were not trick items), whereas students were far less able to correctly identify the trick items.

Here are two of the example trick items from Roberts:

Tricky: A researcher collected some data on 15 students and the mean value was 30 and the standard deviation was .3. What is the sum of X if the variance is 9 and the median is 29?

A. 3
B. 30
C. 15
D. 450

This item is tricky because it is testing trivial content (knowing the sum is the mean times the sample size), but more importantly, it contains irrelevant information about other descriptive statistics.

Tricky: Someone gives a test and also collects some attitude data on a group of parents in a city. The test has an average value of 30 with a variability value of 4 while the attitude average score is 13 with a variance of 18. The relationship between the two variables is .4. What is the regression equation using X to predict Y?

A. $Y = .9 + .2 X$
B. $Y = -32 - 1.3 X$
C. $Y = 3.2 + 3.2 X$
D. None of the above

This item is tricky because of the ambiguity in the stem. Are the test scores X or Y? Is the relationship described by .4 a correlation? Is "variability" the same as variance?

Another example of a tricky item is one similar to an item found in an educational measurement textbook item bank. Consider the following item.

Tricky: A measure of four different social-emotional skills was correlated with high school grades (GPA), with results as shown below. Which measure permits the most accurate prediction of GPA?

A. Positive Identity      $r = +.35$
B. Social Competence    $r = -.20$
C. Mental Distress      $r = -.50$
D. Commitment to Learning   $r = +.40$

This is a tricky item because there are two things being considered in the list. One is the predictor; which predictor of school grades might be most use-ful? We probably believe successful students are committed to learning. Note that positive identity is a strange characteristic, typically meaning self-assured and motivated. And of course we hope that successful students should not be mentally distressed (although it may depend on the school!). But the most accurate prediction is simply a function of the largest correlation, regardless of the direction or sign or the construct being measured. We often think about "prediction" being positive, but statistically, we get more accurate prediction from the correlation with the largest absolute value; it doesn't matter what the predictor is.

### Formatting and Style Concerns

**6.    Format each item vertically instead of horizontally.**

MC items can take up a fair amount of room on a page, especially if there are four or five or more options listed one per line vertically on the page. But this is the preferred formatting, as it avoids potential errors due to formatting the item horizontally, which we sometimes want to do to save room. Consider the following examples:

Poor:    If 64% of the test's total score variance is error variance, what is the test's reliability coefficient?

    A.  .36       B.  .56       C.  .64       D.  .80

Better:    If 64% of the test's total score variance is error variance, what is the test's reliability coefficient?

    A.  .36
    B.  .56
    C.  .64
    D.  .80

In the horizontal format, it's possible to read through the row of letters and numbers and inadvertently select the corresponding letter following the answer choice rather than the letter that precedes it. It can be confusing to tell which letter goes with which option. This is especially possible if the space between options is reduced:

Poor:    Expectancy tables provide what form of validity evidence?

    A. Concurrent    B. Predictive    C. Content    D. Construct

Better:    Expectancy tables provide what form of validity evidence?

    A.    Concurrent
    B.    Predictive
    C.    Content
    D.    Construct

## 7. Edit and proof items.

This should go without saying. If you write items throughout the course of the term, when you start to put them together in a test form, you can review your earlier work and potentially edit items with fresh eyes. Even we occasionally administer class tests that contain typos—often times discovered by students during the exam. This is where we reluctantly get up in front of the class and make the correction announcement, or write the correction on the board. But the best way to ensure limited errors is to have a colleague or teaching assistant review the test before you administer it to the class.

In mathematics and other technical fields, the potential for typographical errors is great. Small errors can indicate very different things. Consider the following:

Poor:    $(2.5 \times 10^{3)}$

Here, the closing parenthesis is in the superscript. Is this supposed to be $(2.5 \times 10^3)$ or is it supposed to be $(2.5 \times 10)^3$?

Poor:    The concepts of reliability and validity of test scores is . . .

Grammar must be consistent ("is" should be "are").

Poor:    Why would a student's local percentile score decrease on a standardized achievement test when the student moved from Minneapolis to Saint Paul?

    A.   Different courses are offered in <u>each</u> district.
    B.   Percentile norms are ordinal measures.
    <u>C.</u>   The ability of the comparison group changed.

The word "each" should not be underlined. If you do underline key words, there should be one underlined in each option. But such writing techniques tend to be distracting and not helpful.

## 8. Keep the language complexity of items at an appropriate level for the class being tested.

This is a challenging guideline. We know from a great deal of research that language complexity often interferes with our ability to measure substantive KSAs. This is particularly important for students with some kinds of disabilities and for students who are nonnative speakers of the language of the test. Unless you are testing language skills and the complexity of reading passages and test questions is relevant to instruction and reflecting the learning objectives, language should be as simple and direct as possible. We don't want unnecessarily complex language in our test items to interfere with our measurement of KSAs in mathematics, science, business, education, or other areas. Even in language-based courses (e.g., literature), the complexity of the language used in test items should be appropriate for the students and reflect the learning objectives.

Poor:    Why would a student's local percentile score attenuate on a standardized achievement test when the student relocated from Minneapolis to Saint Paul?

Unless it was part of the curriculum in the course, the term "attenuate" is not one commonly understood to be synonymous with "decrease." A better version of this stem is provided as an example for guideline #7.

Poor:    What will help ameliorate the negative effects of global warming?
Better:  What will help improve the negative effects of global warming?
Poor:    What is the plausible deleterious result of poor item writing?
Better:  What is the likely harmful result of poor item writing?
Poor:    What would be the result if scientists would put forth effort to promulgate their work?
Better:  When scientists publish their work, they contribute to . . .

Words matter, particularly in diverse classrooms that are likely to include first-generation college students, nonnative speakers of the language of instruction (for most of us, nonnative English speakers), and even students who are not majoring in the field of the course. Terms and language that we might take for granted can make the difference between understanding a question or not. If we want to test for understanding, application, or other higher-order skills, we don't want language to get in the way—unless of course the point of the question is knowledge of language or terminology.

Things to avoid in item writing, unless it is part of the learning objective:

- Technical jargon; use common terms or define special words.
- Passive voice; use active voice.
- Acronyms; spell it out.
- Multiple conditional clauses; be direct and test one condition at a time.
- Adjectives and adverbs; be direct and succinct.
- Abstract contexts; provide concrete examples or contexts.
- Prepositional phrases; if necessary, use only one, and make it important to answering the question.

For more information on creating test items that minimize irrelevant complex language, particularly for nonnative English speakers, see the work of Jamal Abedi (2016), who provides many examples of how language can interfere with measuring KSAs.

## 9.    Minimize the amount of reading in each item. Avoid window dressing.

This is related to but different from the previous guideline on minimizing language complexity. Another way to address the same issue is to reduce the amount of reading in the context materials and test items—unless of course reading is the target of measurement. If the learning objectives are about reading skills and abilities, then the reading load should be appropriate. But in most subject-matter tests, reading skills may interfere with our ability to measure KSAs in the (nonreading) subject matter. Reducing the amount of reading also has the effect of reducing the cognitive load, so that the task presented in the item is focused and allows us to interpret the response as a function of the intended content and cognitive level. In this way, we know how to interpret responses. And it reduces the amount of time required to take the test, possibly making room for additional test items, improving our coverage of the content and learning objectives.

Poor:    Because of the federal education accountability law in the United States of America, known as the Every Student Succeeds Act, every state is required to administer exams to test achievement of reading, mathematics, and science standards. Some states require students to pass one or more of these tests in high school in order to graduate. What makes these high school graduation tests be considered criterion-referenced?

A.   It was built with a test blueprint.
B.   Most students will pass a graduation test.
C.   It is based on a clearly defined domain.
D.   It has a passing score required for graduation.

Better   A high school graduation test is criterion referenced if

A.   it was built with a test blueprint.
B.   most students pass the test.
C.   it is based on a clearly defined domain.
D.   it is required to receive a diploma.

The better version has almost one third the number of words (36 words) compared to the poor version (95 words). Notice that the options are also more direct in the better version.

Poor:    Some current standardized tests report test score results as percentile bands, which include a range of percentile values. One advantage that is claimed for this procedure is that it

A.   expresses results in equal units across the scale.
B.   emphasizes the objective nature of test scores.
C.   reduces the tendency to overinterpret small differences.

Better:   What is one advantage of reporting test results as percentile bands?

A.   They express results in equal units.
B.   They emphasize the objective nature of scores.
C.   They reduce overinterpretation of small differences.

In this case, the number of words was reduced from 51 (poor) to 30 (better). In both cases, the poor versions started with context information that is irrelevant to the target of measurement.

Context is often used in mathematics and science tests, as we want students to be able to apply mathematical and scientific principles in context. But in many cases, the context is not required to solve the problem. If context is used, it must be essential to the question. Otherwise, it introduces irrelevant information that may interfere with measuring the intended learning objective.

Poor:   What is an example of criterion-referenced measurement?

    A.   Santiago's score is three standard deviations above the state mean.
    B.   Hattie scored above the 95th percentile requirement to win the scholarship.
    C.   Jean Luc answered 80 percent of the items correctly.
    D.   Eighty percent of the class scored above a T-score of 55.

Better:   Which phrase represents criterion-referenced measurement?

    A.   80 percent correct
    B.   T-score of 55
    C.   95th percentile

Now, the poor version may be more interesting than the better version, but it does contain irrelevant information and requires more time and effort to read; the number of words was reduced from 48 to 14.

Poor:   Maria José did a study of barriers to student achievement and she measured student test anxiety with a brief questionnaire. She found that most students were similar, with a low amount of anxiety, but there were a few students with extremely high levels of anxiety. Because the anxiety scores were positively skewed, she decided to standardize the scores by transforming them into $z$-scores. What will the shape of the resulting score distribution be?

    A.   Negatively skewed
    B.   Normal
    C.   Positively skewed
    D.   Cannot tell from this information

Better:   If a score distribution is positively skewed, what is the shape of the distribution after the scores are transformed into $z$-scores?

    A.   Negatively skewed
    B.   Normal
    C.   Positively skewed

The fact that Maria José is doing a study of test anxiety is interesting but not needed in order to answer the question. Both versions of this item also have something called a "clang-association" which is described in what follows (guideline 22c), where "positively skewed" appears in the stem and is also one of the options. But in this case, it is an important element of the question. There is a common misconception that standardizing scores also normalizes distributions—which is not true. It would be awkward to avoid this clang association:

Better:   If a score distribution has a heavier right tail, what is the shape of the distribution after the scores are transformed into $z$-scores?

      A.  Negatively skewed
      B.  Normal
      <u>C</u>.  Positively skewed

Introducing "a heavier right tail" also suggests a strange variation in the kurtosis of the distribution rather than a simple focus on skewness. It also requires an additional inference: When one tail is heavier, it is probably skewed. But the focus of the item is on the fact that transforming scores to $z$-scores does not change the shape of the distribution.

### Writing the Stem

**10. Write the stem as a complete question or a phrase to be completed by the options.**

There is some research on this guideline. The evidence suggests that either format is effective for MC items. The following examples illustrate the same item in both formats.

Complete:   What is the difference between the observed score and the error score?

      A.  The derived score
      B.  The standard score
      <u>C</u>.  The true score
      D.  The underlying score

Phrase:   The difference between the observed score and the error score is the

      A.  derived score.
      B.  standard score.
      <u>C</u>.  true score.

Notice that when we use the phrase-completion format, each option starts with a lowercase word and ends with a period. Each option is written so that it completes the stem. We often see other formats that are not appropriate.

Poor:   If 30 out of 100 students answer a question correctly, the item difficulty is:

<u>A.</u>   .30.
B.   .70.
C.   Not enough information is provided to compute item difficulty.

Better:   If 30 out of 100 students answer a question correctly, the item difficulty is

<u>A.</u>   .30.
B.   .70.

Poor:   Internal consistency is a more appropriate form of reliability for:

A.   Criterion-referenced tests
<u>B.</u>   Norm-referenced tests

Better:   Internal consistency is a more appropriate form of reliability for

A.   criterion-referenced tests.
<u>B.</u>   norm-referenced tests.

Ideas for questions or statements for test items can come from many places, including textbook test banks, items in online resources, and course materials, lectures, and discussions. Our most valuable sources of test items are the interactions we have as instructors with our students. Discussions, questions, and comments made during class are full of potential test items. Unfortunately, textbook item banks are not carefully constructed, and often the majority of items contain item-writing flaws. We use textbook item banks as a source for many of the example items in Chapter 6.

> If you use textbook test banks for your test items, be sure to modify the item to be consistent with these guidelines.

## 11. State the main idea in the stem clearly and concisely and not in the options.

The goal is to make the question clear and unambiguous. This is a challenge when the stem is a phrase or part of a statement that is completed in the options. When the item stem does not clearly convey the intended content, too much is left up to the student for interpretation, leaving greater ambiguity in the item and the student's response. In these cases, there are often multiple correct answers, since the distractors are written to be plausible.

Poor:   Percentile norms are

    A.   reported as percentile ranks.
    B.   expressed in interval units of measurement.
    C.   based on a group relevant to the individual.

Better:   In order for norms to provide meaningful information about an individual's performance, they must be

    A.   reported as percentile ranks.
    B.   expressed in interval units of measurement.
    C.   based on a relevant group.

This item also was flawed because the word "percentile" appears in both the stem and the first option. To correct that, we simply removed the word percentile from the stem.

    We've seen examples such as the following four. Each of these shows the entire stem.

Poor:   In the 1970s . . .
          Psychotherapy is . . .
          According to the textbook . . .
          Gender . . .

These stems are simply inadequate and create a great deal of ambiguity and possibly multiple correct options. A good stem is one that allows a student to hypothesize or produce the correct response directly from the stem without reading the options.

## 12. Word the stem positively; avoid negative phrasing.

This guideline has some empirical research behind it. The trouble with negatively worded stems occurs when students overlook the negative word and respond incorrectly because of that rather than responding in a way consistent with their ability. In the health sciences, negatively worded stems are more common and serve an important purpose. In these cases, it is important for the test taker to distinguish among a set of conditions, contexts, symptoms, tests, or related options to identify the one that is *not* appropriate or relevant. In such cases, the negative word should be underlined and in italics and/or bolded, or even in all caps, so the test taker understands what is being asked and doesn't overlook the negative term.

Poor:   What is **NOT** meant by "the test item is highly discriminating"?

    A.   Students who had instruction on the topic are more able to answer it correctly.
    B.   Many more high-ability students than low-ability students answer it correctly.
    C.   It is biased against some groups, as they are less likely to answer it correctly.

Better: What is meant by "the test item is highly discriminating"?

    A.  Only students who had a particular training are able to answer it correctly.

    <u>B.</u>  Many more high-ability students than low-ability students answer it correctly.

    C.  Only a few of the students are able to answer it correctly.

This revised item also is flawed because two of the option start with a common word, "only," making them a pair, and the word "only" is an absolute quantity that is extreme and would rarely be true. Usually this can be corrected by simply removing the word "only."

  Negative phrasing of the stem tends to make items slightly more difficult but also reduces test score reliability—suggesting that it introduces more measurement error in item responses and ultimately in total test scores.

## 13. Move into the stem any words that are repeated in each option.

This helps achieve earlier guidelines by minimizing the amount of reading. Repetitive words are unnecessary and can usually be consolidated in the stem, reducing the amount of reading effort and time for the student.

Poor:   Classical test theory includes the assumption that random error

    A.  is uncorrelated with the observed score.

    <u>B.</u>  is uncorrelated with the true score.

    C.  is uncorrelated with the latent score.

Better: Classical test theory includes the assumption that random error is uncorrelated with the

    A.  observed score.

    <u>B.</u>  true score.

    C.  latent score.

This reduced the number of words from 27 to 19 (a 30% reduction). This adds up quickly across items in a test.

Poor:   What will likely result in a zero discrimination index?

    A.  less able students answer the item correctly

    <u>B.</u>  nearly everyone answers the item correctly

    C.  more able students answer the item correctly

Better: What group of students is more likely to answer the item correctly to produce a zero discrimination index?

A. high ability
<u>B</u>. nearly all
C. low ability

## *Writing the Options*

**14. Write as many options as are needed, given the topic and cognitive task; three options are usually sufficient.**

The quality of the distractors is more important than the number of distractors. But nearly 100 years of experimental research on this topic is unanimous in its finding: Three options is sufficient (Rodriguez, 2005). If three is the optimal number of options, why do most tests have items with four or five options? In large part, this is because of the fear of increasing the chance of randomly guessing correctly. But this same body of research has shown that the effect of guessing does not materialize, particularly in classroom tests and tests that matter to the test taker. Even so, the chance of obtaining a high score on a test of three-option items is relatively low, especially if there are enough items (see Table 4.1).

However, in some cases, four options is the better choice, particularly when trying to achieve balance in the options. Especially for quantitative options, balance can only be achieved by including two positive and two negative options or two odd and two even options or two high and two low options. We shouldn't strive to write three-option items simply for the sake of writing three-option items, especially if it creates an unbalanced set of options. The real goal is to write distractors that are plausible and relevant to the content of the item and that might provide us with feedback about the nature of student errors.

You do not need to use the same number of options for every item. The number of options should reflect the nature of the item, the important plausible distractors, and a single best option. In Chapter 6, nearly all of the example items from various fields have four or five options. A common edit could be

Table 4.1 Chances That a Student Will Score 70% or Higher From Random Guessing

| Number of test items | Chance to score 70% |
| --- | --- |
| 10 | 1 out of 52 |
| 20 | 1 out of 1,151 |
| 30 | 1 out of 22,942 |
| 40 | 1 out of 433,976 |

the reduction of the number of options. Reducing the number of options to three reduces the time required to develop one or two more plausible distractors (see the next guideline) and reduces the reading time for students—particularly reading that is mostly irrelevant to the task at hand. In addition, by reducing the reading time, it's possible to include a few more items and cover the content more thoroughly. This does far more for improving content coverage and the validity of inferences regarding what students know and can do.

## 15. Make all distractors plausible.

To ensure distractors are plausible, they should reflect common misconceptions, typical errors, or careless reasoning. Some of the best distractors are based on uninformed comments that come from students during class discussions or errors students repeatedly make on assignments and other class projects.

Poor:   If we know the exact error of measurement in a student's score and we subtracted this from their observed score, we would obtain the

      A.   ultimate score.
      B.   absolute score.
      <u>C</u>.   true score.

We should be able to justify each distractor as plausible. Here, the distractors are not plausible:

A.   The "ultimate" score is not a term used in measurement.
B.   The "absolute" score is also not a term used in measurement, although the word "absolute" has uses in mathematics, such as absolute values.

Better:   If we know the exact error of measurement in a student's score and we subtracted this from their observed score, we would obtain the

      A.   deviation score.
      B.   standard score.
      <u>C</u>.   true score.

Again, each distractor should be justifiable. Here, the distractors are plausible:

A.   The stem describes a subtraction (observed score minus error), which is also called a deviation. But the deviation score in measurement is the mean score minus the observed score.
B.   A standard score is a type of score in measurement, but it is the difference between scores divided by a standard deviation.

In both distractors, the options are plausible, related to the stem, but not the best answer. Herein we have a great deal of control over the item difficulty. To make the item easier, we could write distractors that are more different (more heterogeneous) but also use real (plausible) scores, such as $T$-score or $z$-score. Similarly, to make items more difficult, we could write distractors that are more similar (more homogeneous), such as the latent score, trait score, or something that is a kind of true score. These other types of scores may be plausible and correct, but only under certain kinds of measurement models that are not described in the item. To make the best option, "true score," the best answer when using even more similar terms as these, it might be necessary to add context to the stem, such as "In Classical Test Theory . . .," making "true score" the only best option.

Poor:    The best way to improve content-related validity evidence for a test is to increase the

      A.   sample size of the validity study.
      <u>B</u>.   number of items on the test.
      C.   amount of time to complete the test.
      D.   statistical power of each item.

Option A contains a word from the stem (validity), which is a clang-association (see guideline 22c) but will result in a more stable score. Option C should improve test score reliability since students will not have to guess if they run out of time. Option D is not plausible since statistical power does not apply to individual items.

Better:   The best way to improve content-related validity evidence for a test is to increase the

      A.   sample of students taking the test.
      <u>B</u>.   number of items on the test.
      C.   amount of time to complete the test.

Now each option will improve the quality of test scores, but only one affects content-related validity evidence.

Many of the example items in Chapter 6 illustrate this guideline. Very few four- or five-option items have three or four plausible distractors.

## 16. Make sure that only one option is the correct answer.

This is a challenge. Make the distractors plausible but not the best answer. The correct option should be unequivocally correct. This is another reason why it is important to have your test reviewed by a colleague, an advanced student, or the teaching assistant.

Poor:    If a raw score distribution is positively skewed, standardizing the scores will result in what type of distribution?

      A.   Normal
      <u>B</u>.   Positively skewed
      C.   Cannot tell from this information

Better:   If a raw score distribution is positively skewed and transformed into z-scores, this will result in what type of distribution?

A.   Normal
<u>B</u>.   Positively skewed
C.   Cannot tell from this information

In the context of what was discussed in class (and in most measurement textbooks), standardizing scores does not change the skewness of the distribution, only the location and spread of the distribution on the score scale. However, there are methods of standardizing scores that are nonlinear, rarely used, but may actually change the shape of the distribution. One such transformation is the normal-curve equivalent (NCE) transformation, which normalizes scores in the transformation, resulting in a normal distribution.

Poor:   In survey research, the set of all possible observations of a social condition is the

A.   frame.
B.   sample.
<u>C</u>.   population.
D.   study.

Option A is also correct, since the sampling frame represents the population available from which to draw the sample. Option D is not of the same kind as the others and is not plausible.

Better:   In survey research, the set of all possible observations of a social condition is the

A.   strata.
B.   sample.
<u>C</u>.   population.

This is one of the most common item-writing flaws we find in textbook item banks. It commonly results from limited knowledge of the subject matter or from hasty item writing. We identify this flaw in the example items in the next chapter. How do we catch such errors? Subject-matter expertise is one step, but even then, peer review is still helpful.

## 17. Place options in logical or numerical order.

In order to avoid clues in how we order the options, particularly the location of the correct option, it is best to be systematic and adopt a simple rule when we order the options. This also helps support the student's thinking and reading clarity. It's distracting and confusing when a list of numbers or dates or names is ordered randomly—without structure. Using logical systems for ordering options reduces cognitive load and allows the student to focus on the important content issues in the item rather than trying to reorder or decipher the order of the options. Not to mention, it's just a nice thing to do.

Poor:   Making judgments about the worth of a program from objective information is called

    A.   validation.
    B.   assessment.
    C.   measurement.
    D.   evaluation.

Better: Making judgments about the worth of a program from objective information is called

    A.   assessment.
    B.   evaluation.
    C.   measurement.
    D.   validation.

Poor =   The proportion of scores less than $z = 0.00$ is

    A.     .00
    B.     1.00
    C.    −.50
    D.     .50

Better: In the unit normal distribution, the proportion of scores less than $z = 0.00$ is

    A.   −.50.
    B.     .00.
    C.     .50.

Notice we also removed one option, 1.00, as this is likely to be the least plausible. In addition to ordering the options numerically, we provided more white space between the letters and the numeric values, so the decimals are not immediately adjacent to each other. When using numbers as options, it is best to align them at the decimal point, again to support the reading effort and to remove additional irrelevant challenges.

Poor:   Which measurement is more precise?

    A.   35.634 meters
    B.   1,152.501 kilometers
    C.   3.823 centimeters

Better: Which measurement is most precise?

    <u>A</u>.       3.823 centimeters
    B.      35.634 meters
    C.  1,152.501 kilometers

There are a few problems with the poor version. First, there are two measurements that are "more" precise than the other. The measurements are not ordered in terms of their magnitudes (centimeters to kilometers), although this might be part of the problem you hope to have students address—but recognize that this does violate the first guideline: Test one aspect of content at a time. But the real issue is the ordering and alignment of the numeric values. The better version eliminates visual challenges and makes the options more accessible to the student.

Poor:   By doubling the sample size in a study, a correlation will most likely

    A.   increase.
    B.   decrease.
    <u>C</u>.   stay the same.

Better:  If the sample size doubles, a correlation will most likely

    A.   decrease.
    <u>B</u>.   stay the same.
    C.   increase.

## 18. Vary the location of the right answer evenly across the options.

The measurement community recommends that each option should be designated to be the correct option about equally often. This is to avoid the tendency to make the middle or the last option correct (which some of us have done). This is also something that many students believe: "If you don't know, guess C!"

    Traditionally, the guideline was to vary the location of the right answer according to the number of options. Tests were often devised so that every item had the same number of options, such as all items having five options. In this case, each options would be correct about 20% (1/5) of the time. But we now know that the number of options should fit the demands of the item, in terms of what's plausible, and also what fits the specific question. So that version of the guideline doesn't really work. We just need to make sure that all options have about the same probability of being correct so that one option is not obviously more likely to be correct.

    By logically or numerically ordering the options, according to guideline 17, we likely avoid these tendencies. But even with this guideline, be sure to check through the key and make adjustments if necessary. Also, we don't want a string of As being correct, or a string of Bs being correct, and so on. We want to mix it up and spread out the correct option across all options. Some students, particularly those who are less prepared, will look for patterns to capitalize on their chances of guessing correctly.

## 19. Keep options independent; options should not overlap.

This is another way of saying: Make sure only one option is the best answer. If the options overlap, then multiple options may be correct.

Poor:   If you are one standard deviation below the mean in a normal distribution, your approximate percentile rank will be

    A.   less than the 10th percentile.
    B.   greater than the 10th percentile.
    <u>C</u>.   greater than the 20th percentile.

Better: If you are one standard deviation below the mean in a normal distribution, your approximate percentile rank will be

    A.   less than the 10th percentile.
    B.   between the 10th and 20th percentiles.
    <u>C</u>.   greater than the 20th percentile.

The problem with the poor version is that B includes C, so both B and C are correct. This issue arises from the use of the term "approximate" in the stem.

Poor:   In item response theory, if a student's ability is at the same level as the location of an item, what is the probability the student will get the item right?

    A.   less than chance
    B.   less than 50%
    <u>C</u>.   about 50%
    D.   greater than 50%

Better: In item response theory, if a student's ability is at the same level as the location of an item, what is the probability the student will get the item right?

    A.   less than 50%
    <u>B</u>.   about 50%
    C.   greater than 50%

In the poor version, A (less than chance) is also part of B (less than 50%). However, there is a more significant technical flaw in this item that only a well-versed item response theory expert will recognize (or a well-read graduate student). The correct answer is 50% for one- and two-parameter IRT models, but not for three-parameter models, in which case the probability of a correct response is greater than 50% (because of the influence of a nonzero lower asymptote).

**20. Avoid using the options *none of the above, all of the above*, and *I don't know*.**

This guideline is one of the most studied empirically. Evidence suggests that it tends to make items slightly less discriminating or less correlated with the total score.

When we use *none of the above* as the correct option, students who may not know the correct answer select this option by recognizing that none of the options is correct. We want students to answer items correctly because they have the KSAs being tapped by the item, not because they know what's not correct.

Poor:   What is NOT a possible modification to a multiple-choice item?

     A.  Requiring students to justify their selected response
     B.  Underlining important words
     C.  Referring to a graphical display
     <u>D.</u>  None of the above

Better: What is a multiple-choice item modification that promotes higher-order thinking?

     <u>A.</u>  Requiring students to justify their selected response
     B.  Underlining important words
     C.  Referring to a graphical display

This is a challenging item. The poor version has a negative term in the stem (NOT) and then in the options (none), creating a double-negative situation. But, more importantly, the question isn't a particularly useful one, since there are potentially many possible modifications to MC items. If a modification is not possible, then it's probably not possible for any items. Even the better option is not ideal, since supporting higher-order thinking depends on the context, and C could also be a correct option for some graphical displays and depending on what is being asked of the student.

When we use *all of the above* as a correct option, students only need to know two of the options are correct, again allowing them to respond correctly with only partial knowledge. If the student recognizes that at least one of the options is incorrect, *all of the above* cannot be the correct option. This option provides clues in both cases, making it a bad choice in item writing.

Poor:   What evidence is useful for building a validity argument about the measurement of a construct?

     A.  Correlations with similar measures
     B.  Mean differences among groups
     C.  Confirmatory factor analysis results
     D.  Expert judgment about item content
     <u>E.</u>  All of the above

Better:  What evidence is useful for building a validity argument about subscore usefulness?

  A.  Correlations with similar measures
  B.  Mean differences among groups
  C.  Confirmatory factor analysis results
  D.  Expert judgment about item content

The problem with the poor version is that a student only needs to know that two of the four options are correct to realize E is the correct answer. Another technical flaw is that, according to Samuel Messick (a prominent validity theorist), all validity evidence supports the construct interpretation of scores.

Finally, you may be tempted to use *I don't know* as an option, but this leaves us without any information about student understanding, since they did not select the option that best reflected their interpretation of the item. If the distractors are common errors or misconceptions, we can obtain diagnostic information about student abilities. The *I don't know* option eliminates this function of testing and wastes our hard effort to develop plausible distractors.

**21. Word the options positively; avoid negative words such as "not."**

We've seen examples already of using negative words in the stem and sometimes in the options. Using negative words in the options simply increases the possibility that students will inadvertently miss the negative term and get the answer wrong, not because of misinformation or lack of knowledge but because of reading too quickly.

Poor:  What is a significant limitation of the multiple-choice item format?

  A.  It is easy to develop many items
  B.  It tends to measure recall
  C.  It takes a long time to read and respond
  D.  It does not allow for innovative responses

Better:  What is the most critical limitation of the multiple-choice item format?

  A.  It is time consuming to develop many items.
  B.  It tends to measure recall.
  C.  It takes a long time to read and respond to.
  D.  It excludes innovative responses.

The poor version has a number of problems. First, it uses a vague quantifier in "a significant limitation." But the primary problem here is the use of NOT within the correct option. First, its use is unique among the options. Moreover, the first option is not a limitation, but it is also not true (since it is challenging to develop many MC items). The better version is still problematic, since all of the options are limitations, so we rely on the clarity of instruction to identify the most critical limitation—we trust that this is clear to students.

Furthermore, when it comes to developing MC items, we argue that the first three options in the better item can be addressed, but the exclusion of innovative responses is nearly impossible to avoid.

## 22. Avoid giving clues to the right answer.

There are several ways that clues can be given to the right answer. These tend to be clues for testwise students—students who are so familiar with testing that they are able to find clues to the correct answer without the appropriate content knowledge. The six most common clues are included here.

## 22a. Keep the length of options about equal.

This guideline has been studied empirically. The evidence consistently indicates that making the correct option longer makes items easier (due to it providing a clue to the correct answer) and significantly reduces validity (correlations with other similar measures).

The most common error committed by classroom teachers and college instructors is to make the correct option longer than the distractors. We tend to make the correct option longer by including details that help us defend its correctness. Testwise students recognize that the longest option is often the correct option.

Poor:   The major difference between teacher-made and standardized achievement tests is in their

    A.  relevance to specific instructional objectives for a specific course.
    B.  item difficulty.
    C.  item discrimination.
    D.  test score reliability.

Better: What is the major difference between teacher-made and standardized tests?

    A.  blueprints
    B.  item difficulties
    C.  number of items
    D.  score reliabilities

The wording on this guideline is deliberate. The options don't need to be exactly the same length, which is not practical. They just need to be "about equal." There should not be noticeably large differences in option length.

**22b. Avoid specific determiners including "always," "never," "completely," and "absolutely."**

Words such as "always," "never," "all," "none," and others that are specific and extreme are rarely, if ever, true. These words clue testwise students, who know that these terms are rarely defensible.

Poor:   In general, the test item that is more likely to have a zero discrimination index is the one that

  A.   all the less able students get correct.
  B.   nearly everyone gets correct.
  C.   all the more able students get correct.

Better:   In general, the test item that is more likely to have a zero discrimination index is the one that

  A.   low-ability students are more likely to get correct.
  B.   nearly all students get correct.
  C.   high-ability students are more likely to get correct.

The poor version has at least two issues. One is that A and C use the term "all." Second, A and C present a pair of options, since they have the same structure, which is different than B. This second issue is still somewhat of a problem in the better item.

Poor:   One benefit of learning more about educational measurement is that

  A.   people have respect for measurement specialists.
  B.   it brings complete credibility to our work.
  C.   it improves our teaching and assessment practice.
  D.   teachers generally have little assessment literacy.

Better:   One benefit of learning more about educational measurement is that

  A.   it brings some credibility to our work.
  B.   it improves our teaching and assessment practice.
  C.   teachers generally have little assessment literacy.

Here, the poor version includes "complete" in option B, which was changed to "some" in the better version. Also, option A in the poor version is probably not true (especially these days with the negative environment around testing) and is likely the least plausible option, so it was removed.

This is also a common flaw for true-false items. Here, the term "only" is too difficult to justify, potentially leading students to select false.

Poor:   According to social exchange theory, trust is the only factor needed to maintain relationships. (True or False)

Better: According to social exchange theory, trust is more important than the ratio between costs and benefits to maintain relationships. (True or <u>False</u>)

**22c. Avoid clang associations, options identical to or resembling words in the stem.**

Another clue to testwise students (most students actually) is when a word that appears in the stem also appears in one or more options. This is also a problem when a different form or version of the same word appears in both the stem and an option. There were multiple examples of this in some of the other item-writing guidelines, including example items for guidelines 9 and 15 (it's a common error).

A clang association is a speech characteristic of some psychiatric patients. It is the tendency to choose words because of their sound not their meaning. Sometimes the choice of words is because of rhyming or the beginning sound of the words. This is associated to another disorder psychiatrists call the "word salad," a random string of words that do not make sense but might sound interesting together. We don't want items to contain clang associations or take the form of a word salad!

The key point here is that we don't want students to select options or discredit options because of a similar word or words that sound the same in the stem and the options.

Poor:   What can we use to report content-related validity evidence for test interpretation?

    A.   Reliability coefficients
    B.   Validity coefficients
    <u>C</u>.   The test blueprint
    D.   Think-aloud studies

Better: What can we use to report content-related validity evidence for test interpretation?

    A.   Criterion correlations
    B.   Reliability coefficients
    <u>C</u>.   The test blueprint
    D.   Think-aloud studies

The poor version contains the term "validity" in both the stem and option B. In addition, in the poor version, options A and B present a pair (see guideline 22d), since they are both "coefficients." All of the distractors are forms of validity evidence, but only C directly addresses the content of the test.

**22d. Avoid pairs or triplets of options that clue the test taker to the correct choice.**

When two or three options are similar in structure, share common terms, or are similar in other ways, students can often see which options to eliminate or which options might be correct.

Poor:    Concepts about validity have continuously evolved for decades. The prevailing conceptualization of validity in educational measurement suggests that it is

     A.   a property of the test.
     B.   a unitary characteristic of the test.
     C.   a subjective decision.
     <u>D.</u>   a property of score interpretation.

Better:  The educational measurement validity framework described by Kane includes a focus on

     A.   decisions about test content.
     <u>B.</u>   test score interpretation.
     C.   internal structure of the test.

The poor version has a number of problems, including the pair of options in A and B, both about the test itself, and "property" and "characteristic" are synonyms. If you know one is wrong, you know the other is wrong. In addition, the first sentence of the stem is unnecessary—window dressing. Also, in the better version, the distractors A and B are both forms of validity evidence but not the focus of validity itself.

Other examples of option pairs can be found in the example items presented in guidelines 12, 22b, and 22c.

## 22e. Avoid blatantly absurd, ridiculous, or humorous options.

There is no experimental research on this topic, but it has been written about. Berk (2000) found evidence that humor can reduce anxiety, tension, and stress in the college classroom. The bulk of the research on humor in testing has occurred in undergraduate psychology classes. The results regarding the effects of humor in testing to reduce anxiety and stress were mixed. Berk conducted a set of experiments using humorous test items and measuring anxiety among students in an undergraduate statistics course. Students reported that the use of humor in exams was effective in reducing anxiety and encouraging their best performance on the exam. Here are some examples of how Berk illustrated his recommendations to use humor in the stem or in the options.

Example 1:  The artist formerly known as MS-DOS is

       A.   Linux.
       B.   X Window.
       <u>C.</u>   Windows.
       D.   Unix.
       E.   Mac OS.

Example 2:   What is the most appropriate politically correct term for *ex-spouse* (not necessarily yours)?

        A.   cerebrally challenged
        B.   parasitically oppressed
        C.   insignificant other
        D.   socially misaligned

Another example he provided is for the matching format, and although it is not an MC item format, it is a humorous example of how this guideline can be applied to other formats. This is slightly modified from the item presented by Berk (2000).

Example 3:   Match each questionnaire item with the highest level of measurement it captures. Mark your answer on the line preceding each item. Each level of measurement may be used once, more than once, or not at all.

| *Questionnaire Item* | *Level of Measurement* |
| --- | --- |
| _B_ Wait time to see your doctor | |
| ☐ 10 minutes or less | A. Nominal |
| ☐ more than 10 but less than 30 minutes | B. Ordinal |
| ☐ between 30 minutes and 1 hour | C. Interval |
| ☐ more than 1 hour and less than 1 day | D. Ratio |
| ☐ I'm still waiting | |
| _B_ Degree of frustration | |
| ☐ Totally give up | |
| ☐ Might give up | |
| ☐ Thinking about giving up | |
| ☐ Refuse to give up | |
| ☐ Don't know the meaning of "give up" | |
| _D_ Scores on the "Where's Waldo" final exam (0–100) | |
| _A_ Symptoms of exposure to statistics | |
| ☐ Vertigo | |
| ☐ Nausea | |
| ☐ Vomiting | |
| ☐ Numbness | |
| ☐ Hair loss | |
| _D_ Quantity of blood consumed by Dracula per night (in ml) | |

Berk (2000) wisely recommended evaluating the use of humor if you decide to use it in your tests. He suggested giving a brief anonymous survey to students, including questions such as:

1.   Did you like the humorous items on the test?
2.   Were they too distracting?
3.   Did they help you perform your best on the test?

4. Should humorous items be included on the next test?
5. Do you have any comments about the use of humor on class tests?

We recognize that Berk himself is a very humorous writer and measurement specialist. He is known for taking complex materials and controversial topics and making them understandable through humor. Think about how many social controversies have been clarified through cartoons (especially political cartoons). Sometimes it works. But we also recognize that one person's humor may not be so humorous to another. We adopt the guidelines of McMorris, Boothroyd, and Pietrangelo (1997), who did an earlier review of research on the use of humor in testing. They recommended that if humor is used in testing, the following conditions should be ensured:

1. It is consistent with the use of humor during instruction and class activities.
2. The test has no time limit, or a very generous one.
3. The humor is positive, avoids sensitive content, and is appropriate for the group.
4. The item writer (instructor) understands the cultural contexts of all students.
5. It should be used sparingly and not count against students' performance.

**22f. Keep options homogeneous in content and grammatical structure.**

When options cover a variety of content, it becomes easier to detect the correct answer, even without much content knowledge. Similarly, a common clue to students is inconsistent or incorrect grammar. These are common item-writing flaws that can be avoided through good editing and review of the test items by peers.

   This can also be an effective way to control item difficulty. As described in the section on item difficulty that follows, the extent to which options are similar and homogenous often determines the difficulty of the task presented to students.

Poor:   What information does the mean score provide?

   A. The spread of scores on the score scale
   B. The shape of the score distribution
   C. The location of the distribution on the score scale

Better:   What information does the mean score provide?

   A. Where most of the scores are concentrated
   B. The value of the most common score
   C. The location of the distribution on the score scale

The poor version includes distractors that are related to score distributions but not to central tendency—A is about variability and B is about shape. In the better version, the two distractors are both about central tendency.

Items with absurd options also violate this guideline, since they are not homogenous with the other options. But the degree to which options are absurd can be subjective, sometimes including options that are just not plausible.

Poor:   In what year was Ronald Reagan elected?

    A.   1971
    B.   1984
    C.   1979
    D.   2000

This item has a number of problems. First, Ronald Reagan was elected to the governorship of California twice (1970s) and the presidency twice (1980s)—so which is the question asking about? Second, these are not all election years. There is a difference between when one is elected and when one takes office. Third, the years are not in order. Fourth, 2000 is not plausible for students who are studying the national leadership timeline. Finally, this item is tapping simple recall and is not particularly informative.

Better:   Which Ronald Reagan election was considered a landslide?

    A.   1967 election as California governor
    B.   1971 reelection as California governor
    C.   1980 election as U.S. president
    D.   1984 reelection as U.S. president

## Can We Control Item Difficulty?

We now see that there are many elements of MC items that may contribute to difficulty. However, in classroom tests, we want item difficulty to be a natural reflection of the cognitive demands of the curriculum. In standardized testing, we typically want items with a wide range of difficulty to assess the KSAs of students across the full ability continuum. But in classroom assessment, assuming that students have had the opportunity to learn the content material and have made some effort to learn it, a large percentage of students should display mastery of the content on the test. Content mastery is, after all, the goal of instruction and the typical purpose for most courses.

### Consider How Difficult a Test Item Might Be

Some measurement specialists have argued that for classroom assessments, the target for item difficulty should be about .70—that is, about 70% of the students should get an item correct. This may be a result of the conventional (yet unfounded) wisdom that "70% is passing." However, this fails to account for the nature of the content, the quality of instruction and learning opportunities, and the purpose of the test—areas in which you now have much more expertise.

More important is our ability to write items that help us distinguish between students who have mastered the content materials and those who have not. We want to develop items so that students with the KSAs will answer the item correctly and students with misconceptions, misinformation, problem-solving errors, and the like will answer the item incorrectly. If everyone has learned the topic or issue presented in a given item, then the item $p$-value should be 1.0. If all of the students retain misconceptions or make a common error in solving a problem, then the item $p$-value should be 0.0. But in all cases, each item should cover important and relevant content.

As described, we can manipulate the difficulty of MC items most effectively through the development and selection of distractors (incorrect options). The selection of distractors should capture common misconceptions, misinformation, and problem-solving errors. In addition, when distractors are plausible and closely related to the key, we can create items that distinguish students with deeper understanding while assessing important abilities to parse important nuances of KSAs.

## Applications

This chapter described the general process of developing MC items, with recommendations on item structure and selection of tested content. MC item-writing guidelines were then provided, with poor and better examples for each one. In these exercises, you will apply your understanding of the guidelines by using them to write and evaluate MC items.

1.  Reflect on MC items you've written in the past. What guidelines from this chapter have you found to be important? What guidelines have been difficult to follow? How can your items be improved?
2.  Explain to a peer how each guideline can improve the quality of an item. Share your own examples of guideline violations.
3.  Write new MC questions according to the test blueprint you developed in Chapter 3. Remember to target the appropriate cognitive task by referencing novel material and contexts.
4.  Review and give feedback on the MC questions of a peer. Pay close attention to consistency of wording and content in the options and the plausibility of the distractors.

## References

Abdulghani, H. M., Ahmad, F., Irshad, M., Khalil, M. S., Al-Shaikh, G. K., Syed, S., Aldrees, A. A., Alrowais, N., and Haque, S. (2015). Faculty development programs improve the quality of multiple choice questions items' writing. *Scientific Reports*, 5(9556), 1–7.

Abedi, J. (2016). Language issues in item development. In S. Lane, M.R. Raymond, and T.M. Haladyna (Eds.), *Handbook of test development* (2nd ed., pp. 355–373). New York, NY: Routledge.

Berk, R.A. (2000). Does humor in course tests reduce anxiety and improve performance? *College Teaching*, 48(4), 151–158.

Downing, S.M. (2005). The effects of violating standard item writing principles on tests and students: The consequences of using flawed test items on achievement examinations in medical education. *Advances in Health Sciences Education*, 10, 133–143.

Haladyna, T.M., and Rodriguez, M.C. (2013). *Developing and validating test items*. New York, NY: Routledge.

Jozefowicz, R.F., Koeppen, B.M., Case, S., Galbraith, R., Swanson, D., and Glew, R.H. (2002). The quality of in-house medical school examinations. *Academic Medicine*, 77(2), 156–161.

McMorris, R.F., Boothroyd, R.A., and Pietrangelo, D.J. (1997). Humor in educational testing: A review and discussion. *Applied Measurement in Education*, 10(3), 269–297.

Naeem, N., van der Vleuten, C., and Alfaris, E.A. (2012). Faculty development on item writing substantially improves item quality. *Advances in Health Science Education*, 17, 369–376.

Roberts, D.M. (1993). An empirical study on the nature of trick test questions. *Journal of Educational Measurement*, 30(4), 331–344.

Rodriguez, M.C. (2005). Three options are optimal for multiple-choice items: A meta-analysis of 80 years of research. *Educational Measurement: Issues and Practice*, 24(2), 3–13.

Tarrant, M., Knierim, A., Hayes, S.K., and Ware, J. (2006). The frequency of item writing flaws in multiple-choice questions used in high stakes nursing programs. *Nurse Education Today*, 26(8), 662–671.

Tarrant, M., and Ware, J. (2008). Impact of item-writing flaws in multiple-choice questions on student achievement in high-stakes nursing assessments. *Medical Education*, 42, 198–206.

# 5 Getting Practice and Feedback Online

A variety of tools are available to you for practicing and learning about item writing and test development and building your course tests. This chapter reviews some of these tools, with an emphasis on Proola, a web application developed, in part, to accompany this book. The Proola resources introduced here will allow you to apply and extend your learning about effective item writing through sharing and collaboration with peers.

## Chapter Learning Objectives

1. Describe the basic structure and common uses of a learning-management system, and identify the system used by your college or university.
2. Summarize the resources available to you for building a course test, including published item banks and resources from a local teaching and learning center, and identify the strengths and limitations of these resources.
3. Navigate the basic features of Proola so as to create instructional learning objectives and write items addressing these objectives.
4. Revise your items to improve their match to learning objectives and appropriate cognitive tasks and to fix any item-writing flaws.
5. Utilize the item-writing guidelines and principles of effective test development to evaluate and give constructive feedback on the items of peers.

## What Is a Learning-Management System?

As an instructor, you've probably used learning-management systems (LMS) in one way or another to manage data or information on students in a course you teach. An LMS is software that helps you organize and share course content with students and collect data from students in the form of assessments, assignments, and other submitted work. An LMS also provides tools for communication and collaboration between you and students and among students. LMSs differ from other computer-based instructional resources in their scope. LMSs are intended to be a comprehensive solution addressing all aspects of the teaching and learning processes, whereas other resources may only address certain components of these processes. Some popular examples of LMSs include Black-board, Moodle, and Canvas by Instructure.

LMSs provide a number of resources to support the development of course tests. Features are available for creating and storing a variety of item types, administering items to students, and evaluating item quality with metrics such as item difficulty and discrimination (more on these in Chapter 7). Features are also available for sharing items with other instructors and accessing item banks from textbook publishers (more on this in what follows). LMSs provide only limited support for improving the quality of your own items or evaluating available items.

## What Item-Writing Tools Are Available?

As you probably know, course textbooks in higher education commonly provide access to item banks, sets of example test items that are intended to assess student KSAs related to the content of the textbook. These item banks may be printed within an instructor's copy of the textbook or given in a separate publication as a supplement to the textbook itself. Many are now provided electronically, with some being integrated into LMSs through add-ons from textbook publishers. In the next chapter, we review numerous items from sources such as these.

The quality of items in textbooks or LMS item banks should not be taken for granted. Instead, these resources should be used as starting points when creating your own course test. Published example items can demonstrate both effective and ineffective ways of assessing the KSAs in your instructional learning objectives. Most often, these items will be flawed in at least one way and will need to be modified to meet the item-writing guidelines in Chapter 4 and to address the content and cognitive tasks established in your test blueprint based on your learning objectives. Reusing example items without editing and adaption can result in tests measuring unbalanced or irrelevant content, which can lead to invalid score interpretations for your students.

Valuable local resources for improving your item-writing skills and the quality of your test items are often provided by a teaching and learning center at your college or university. Examples with links are provided in Chapter 2. Proola was developed to supplement these resources by providing educators with an online learning community and shared space for practicing writing items.

## An Overview of Proola

Proola was originally developed as a resource for educational and psychological measurement courses, where graduate students were required to write and comment on the test items of their peers. The site proola.org provides a simple interface for creating MC and SR questions and then tracking conversations about these questions as they are revised and improved. Proola is continuously being developed to support different audiences of item writers and test developers, including K–12 teachers and college and university instructors. Access is free but requires registration at proola.org/signup.

After signing up for an account, you'll have access to the item bank and a user dashboard, where you can store and organize your learning objectives, test blueprints, items, and tests. The item bank contains all of the items that have been submitted for review and peer feedback. Note that items from your specific field may not yet be available.

Proola differs from other item-banking and assessment-sharing software in two main ways. First, it is primarily intended to support learning about assessment. Proola does not currently support administering and collecting student responses on assessments. Instead, it aims to be a sandbox for writing items while building item-writing skills. Items created in Proola can easily be exported to PDF or to an LMS for administration. Second, Proola functions as a community of educators and measurement specialists in which knowledge and quality assessments are built collaboratively via peer review.

### The Proola Item Bank

The item bank at proola.org/items gives you access to hundreds of items written by students and educators with various backgrounds and levels of experience in assessment and measurement. Searching the bank, you may not find items that address your own instructional objectives. However, you will find items from a variety of subjects that demonstrate common mistakes in the item-writing process. You'll also find items that adhere to the guidelines and incorporate novel contexts to assess higher cognitive tasks. Items of different qualities can serve as examples for you as you brainstorm effective methods for assessing your own course content.

As you browse the bank, you'll notice that users can comment on others' items. You should read through others' comments before providing comments of your own (more on commenting in what follows). You'll also notice that you can save others' items. Once saved, they'll show up in your dashboard for easy access.

### The Peer-Review Process

As we noted, Proola is built around a simple model of peer review. Before an item is designated as "Approved" in the item bank, it must have been submitted and available in the bank for commenting, and it must have received a formal review, with a positive result, from a Proola administrator. Once you have created your learning objectives, the review process for items involves four main steps:

1.  Draft your item using a simple interface. Link to one or more appropriate learning objectives.

2.  Get feedback from friends and local support. While an item is in draft status, you select who gets to access it, whether everyone or other users in select groups.
3.  Edit your draft item based on any feedback you receive. In your revisions, focus on the item-writing guidelines and your selected learning objective(s). Aim for the highest appropriate cognitive task. Double-check for clarity and correct spelling and grammar.
4.  Submit your item for review to share with the community. After submitting an item, there's no turning back. You and others can still comment, but edits are locked until a formal peer review is complete.

Peer review will be provided by a Proola administrator, and results will show up within the conversation below the latest draft of your item. If revisions are recommended, you'll have the opportunity to revise and resubmit. Any edits will then be made to a new version of the item, where previous versions are viewable but not editable. The revision process can be repeated as needed until the fourth version of the item. Once approved, your item can be printed and exported by other users, and you begin to build recognition with the community as an effective item writer.

### Authoring Items

Here we provide some pointers on authoring your own learning objectives and corresponding test items in Proola. Before you begin, you should browse the objectives and items of other users for examples of what to do and what not to do. That said, don't be afraid to make mistakes, as you can always edit and delete what you don't like up until you submit your work for peer review.

Item development begins with the development of a clear and concise instructional learning objective (see Chapter 2 for guidelines). In Proola, you can create and store objectives in your user dashboard and submit them for peer review prior to beginning item writing. Here are some guidelines on writing effective objectives.

•   Start with course objectives. These will tie into units and possibly sub-units of instruction in your course. Often, units correspond to chapters or parts of a textbook. Your course objectives will provide a broad structure to your instructional objectives. Course objectives can be saved in your Proola dashboard.
•   Instructional objectives should directly reference the content that matters. It's best not to work backward, writing an objective to match an existing item. Instead, work from the ground up. Visit the content for a particular unit in your course and identify a component of the unit that can be expressed in terms of a measureable student outcome.
•   Instructional objectives are best designed in groups. If you write an objective and one or more items to assess it and then move on to

writing another objective, you may find yourself revising the same material or writing objectives that overlap. Your objectives should be distinct from one another. Creating them in sets will help limit redundancies.

- Don't shy away from revising your objectives. You should revisit your objectives each time you reteach a course and revise them as needed to reflect updates in the content. This will necessarily require a realignment and potential rewriting of your test items.

Once your objectives have been revised as needed, you can start working on items that address them. The item-writing process is simple. Proola requires that you provide a brief descriptive title for your item, along with a target grade level and subject area. Then your item consists of a stem and at least one option. Follow the item-writing guidelines given in Chapter 4 while keeping in mind the following points.

- Whereas objectives are best written and organized in groups or sets, individual items need not be associated with a specific test or quiz. However, each item should be associated with a primary learning objective. If you find yourself assessing multiple objectives in a single item, you may need to simplify the item content and cognitive task.
- Focus on content over formatting. Write the item text first, and then format, as needed, second. Proola does provide basic formatting tools; however, these should be used sparingly. Instead, the content should speak for itself as much as possible.
- Finally, if you aren't ready to write objectives and items for your own course content, try writing items to existing objectives from this book.

### Reviewing Others' Work

Reviewing and commenting on the work of others will give you a new perspective on the item-development process. By participating in peer review, you'll learn new item-writing strategies, such as using applications to assess higher depth of knowledge and cognitive tasks. You'll also see approaches that should be avoided, such as making an item difficult via trickery (intentionally writing an item to catch the distracted student). Here are a few principles of effective commenting.

- Be constructive. Comments will naturally flow toward the limitations of an objective or item. Remember to highlight strengths as well as weaknesses, and always provide suggestions for improvement.
- Reference the guidelines. Flawed items tend to miss one or more item-writing guidelines. Organize and focus your comments by referring to the guidelines. A dropdown in the commenting area gives you easy access to the list.

- Target objectives and cognitive tasks. Always check scope, that is, how well items address the intended instructional objective(s) at the appropriate cognitive task or depth of knowledge.

## Applications

1.   Add the instructional learning objectives you developed in Chapter 2 to Proola. After reviewing objectives from other users, refine yours and then submit them for peer review.
2.   Upload to Proola the MC items you wrote in Chapter 4. Review other users' items, revise your own based on what you learn, and then submit for peer review.
3.   Review the learning objectives and items of a peer. Highlight a balance of strengths and weaknesses. Provide suggestions for improvement to address any flaws you identify.
4.   Take the item development assessment on Proola. What content have you mastered? What guidelines or item flaws did you struggle to identify or address? Based on your results, make a plan to address any gaps in your KSAs.

# 6 Example Items From Various Fields

Test items were collected from test banks associated with college textbooks in many fields. These include

- Business: 15 items
- Health Sciences: 23 items
- Statistics: 19 items
- Sciences: 20 items
- Social Sciences: 39 items

Some of the items in this chapter were provided by instructors using Proola, by us (Drs. Rodriguez and Albano, referred to as authors), and faculty colleagues (referred to as faculty), but many were obtained from college textbook test banks and reproduced with permission as noted.

In our search for example items, we found several online resources that are rich reservoirs of items available for others to use. Certainly there are others and likely many more to come. In addition to the growing item banks in Proola, there is a growing number of sites to explore. This also includes websites developed by faculty who choose to make their course materials and test questions freely available online, outside learning-management systems that are typically open only to students enrolled in a course. Here we provide just a small sample of those sites we explored, including a brief description of what can be found at each.

## Help Teaching

- A site that is primarily devoted to providing test items, activities, lessons, and games for K–12 teachers, tutors, trainers, and homeschool parents. However, there are resources for college instructors. The site contains nearly 9,000 test questions at the college level across various subject areas.
- Select the "Category" for a subject area; "Grades" for College, Graduate, or Continuing Education level; and "Question Types" and it will provide you with access to many items.
- www.helpteaching.com/search/advanced.htm

### Advanced Placement Exams

- The College Board has been in the testing business for decades and has provided access to AP exam information, including previous forms of AP exams and lots of example items. These are college-level items that are well developed, including items that measure higher-order thinking and complex cognitive tasks.
- http://apcentral.collegeboard.com/apc/public/exam/exam_information/index.html

### Biology 121, Missouri State

- As an example of what some professors are willing to provide, Dr. Barnhart posts his lecture slides, practice exams, and other resources for his courses, including biology. His exam items are clear and direct. We obtained permission to reproduce a few and offer modest suggestions for improvement. But the vast majority of the items he provides are well developed.
- http://courses.missouristate.edu/ChrisBarnhart/bio121/

### A Caution

We also provide a cautionary note on the wide availability of online sharing and social networking sites. Students can post course materials, including exams, without the knowledge of the instructor. A few moments of searching may uncover materials from your department or institution and possibly even your course. One such site is *Koofers*, a site that provides free access to test banks, course exams, course content flashcards, and other resources for students. Consistent with the traditional practices of student governments, fraternities and sororities, and other campus organizations, it allows members to post tests for others to access. You can search for specific colleges and universities and then subject area to see if students have posted specific course materials.

Related to this, there are multiple sites online that provide access to test banks associated with college textbooks, typically for a price, but many provide limited free access. This was recently seen in the University of Central Florida case in which students obtained the test bank for their business course and studied from it—only to find out that the midterm exam in the course was based on items from the test bank. This has fueled new debates on college campuses regarding the often-blurry line around what constitutes cheating.

### YOUR TASK

1. Consider the items in the following sections. You may start with the subject area with which you are most familiar.

2. Challenge yourself and review items in other areas—perhaps those in which you are less familiar.

3. Identify the item-writing flaws in each item. Each item has at least one feature that can be improved. Record the item-writing guideline that may be used to improve the item.

4. Also, consider offering improvements to the item.

5. At the end of the chapter, we provide a list of specific item-writing guidelines that might be used to improve each of these sample items. Check this list to see if you identified a similar set of guidelines that might be used to improve each item—although there may be others.

We do not intend to criticize any particular textbook author(s), item writers, or publishers. We fully recognize that item writing is difficult and have offered many of our own classroom test items in previous chapters that were in dire need of editing or revision.

There are volumes of research on the quality of existing test items, including items on high-stakes tests of academic achievement, college admissions tests, and certification and licensure exams. Even the most seasoned item writer will produce items that turn out to be less than optimal—or downright defective.

The items written for textbook test banks are a great resource for college instructors. And, as we've described in Chapters 4 and 5, they should be edited or modified to fit the content and learning objectives of your particular course. Remember, the vast majority of these items have not been field tested or reviewed by measurement specialists, let alone psychometricians. In this book, you have the results of a rare and intensive review of dozens of items from multiple fields and subjects.

## Business

### *Managing Quality*

1. People view quality subjectively and in relation to differing criteria based on their individual roles in the production-marketing value chain. <u>True</u>/False

> From Evans. *Managing for Quality and Performance Excellence*, 9E.
> © 2014 South-Western, a part of Cengage Learning, Inc.
> Reproduced by permission. www.cengage.com/permissions

2. Although quality can drive business success, it cannot guarantee it, and one must not infer that business failures or stock price drops are the result of poor quality. <u>True</u>/False

> From Evans. *Managing for Quality and Performance Excellence*, 9E.
> © 2014 South-Western, a part of Cengage Learning, Inc.
> Reproduced by permission. www.cengage.com/permissions

3.  The quality assurance team in a firm is solely responsible for ensuring that the products produced meet the required quality specifications. True/<u>False</u>

> From Evans. *Managing for Quality and Performance Excellence*, 9E.
> © 2014 South-Western, a part of Cengage Learning, Inc.
> Reproduced by permission. www.cengage.com/permissions

4.  The book "Quality Is Free" is written by _____.
    <u>a</u>.  Philip Crosby
    b.  Edwards Deming
    c.  Malcolm Baldrige
    d.  Joseph Juran

> From Evans. *Managing for Quality and Performance Excellence*, 9E.
> © 2014 South-Western, a part of Cengage Learning, Inc.
> Reproduced by permission. www.cengage.com/permissions

## Human Resource Management

5.  Which is not one of the major challenges currently facing HR managers?
    <u>a</u>.  motivating employees without pay raises and promotion
    b.  changing federal, state and local legal requirements
    c.  adjusting benefit programs due to increasing costs
    d.  replacing "baby boomers" as they exit the workplace

> From Mathis/Jackson. *Human Resource Management*, 13E.
> © 2011 South-Western, a part of Cengage Learning, Inc.
> Reproduced by permission. www.cengage.com/permissions

6.  Human resource management is
    a.  supervising, monitoring, controlling, and disciplining employees in order to achieve organizational goals efficiently and effectively.
    <u>b</u>.  the designing of organizational systems to ensure that human talent is used effectively and efficiently to accomplish organizational goals.
    c.  the efficient and effective use and coordination of human capital to ensure the profitability and long-term sustainability of the organization.
    d.  the design of the interface between the human capital of the firm and its technological and financial capital in order to efficiently and effectively reach organizational goals.

> From Mathis/Jackson. *Human Resource Management*, 13E.
> © 2011 South-Western, a part of Cengage Learning, Inc.
> Reproduced by permission. www.cengage.com/permissions

7. _____ identifies paths and activities for individual employees as they develop within the organization.
   a. Staffing
   b. HR development
   c. Equal Employment Opportunity
   d. Career planning

   > From Mathis/Jackson. *Human Resource Management*, 13E.
   > © 2011 South-Western, a part of Cengage Learning, Inc.
   > Reproduced by permission. www.cengage.com/permissions

8. The shared values and beliefs of an organization is its
   a. social network.
   b. ethical environment.
   c. intellectual capital.
   d. organizational culture.

   > From Mathis/Jackson. *Human Resource Management*, 13E.
   > © 2011 South-Western, a part of Cengage Learning, Inc.
   > Reproduced by permission. www.cengage.com/permissions

9. Which of the following statements about organizational culture is FALSE?
   a. The organization's culture is seen in its norms of expected behaviors, values, philosophies, rituals and symbols.
   b. An organization's rules of behavior may not be beneficial and may limit the organization's performance.
   c. Organizational cultures are static, and tend to remain almost identical to the culture established by the founder.
   d. Values determine how organizational members treat coworkers and people outside the organization.

   > From Mathis/Jackson. *Human Resource Management*, 13E.
   > © 2011 South-Western, a part of Cengage Learning, Inc.
   > Reproduced by permission. www.cengage.com/permissions

10. Organizational productivity for the local Meals on Wheels charity ultimately affects the organization's
    a. total costs.
    b. profitability.
    c. total revenue.
    d. competitiveness.

    > From Mathis/Jackson. *Human Resource Management*, 13E.
    > © 2011 South-Western, a part of Cengage Learning, Inc.
    > Reproduced by permission. www.cengage.com/permissions

**Business Research**

11. The RFP process is one through which a business can invite research firms to propose research designs and plans to provide information to promote the goals of the business. What is an RFP?
    A.  response from promoters
    B.  request for proposal
    C.  research firm proposition
    D.  required future plan
    Source: Faculty

12. The goal of effective business research is to gather
    A.  useful information.
    B.  evidence of effectiveness.
    C.  the truth.
    D.  real opinions.
    E.  all of the above.
    Source: Faculty

13. Full-service research firms should employ research specialists that have a wide range of skills, including sampling specialists in order to
    A.  conduct statistical analyses.
    B.  facilitate focus groups.
    C.  design probability samples.
    D.  produce professional reports.
    Source: Faculty

14. Business research
    A.  should impact employee policies.
    B.  support sound business decision making.
    C.  needs to be mixed-methods to be practical.
    D.  cannot be simulated.
    Source: Faculty

15. There are multiple steps in the business research process. Where one starts depends on the need for information and where the business is at regarding its own research experience.
    A.  Before any research begins, it's critical to create a decision statement.
    B.  Exploratory research requires an experimental design with a control group.
    C.  Results of primary research have clear and direct application to practice.
    D.  Research is actually a waste of funds, since product quality is all that matters.
    Source: Faculty

# Health Sciences

## *Pharmacology*

1. The student is providing a presentation to the class regarding concepts in pharmacodynamics. Which statement made by a student in the class best demonstrates understanding of pharmacodynamics?
   a. "Excretion and metabolism are components of pharmacodynamics."
   b. "Receptor binding is the main component of pharmacodynamics."
   c. "Age and gender are components of pharmacodynamics."
   d. "Routes of administration are components of pharmacodynamics."

   This item was published in the Test Bank for *Pharmacology for Nursing Care*, 7th ed., Lehne, Chapter 1: Orientation to Pharmacology, p. 1. Copyright Elsevier (2010).

2. What government agency or agencies control(s) prescription or legend medications?
   a. Drug Enforcement Agency
   b. Bureau of Dangerous Drugs
   c. Food and Drug Administration
   d. a and c
   e. all of the above

   This item was published in the Test Bank for *Pharmacology*, 2nd ed., Fulcher, Fulcher, and Soto, Chapter 1: Legal and Ethical Aspects of Pharmacology, p. 1. Copyright Elsevier (2009).

3. The act that allows drug manufacturers to find new uses in rare medical conditions for medications previously found to be dangerous is the
   a. Controlled Substances Act of 1970
   b. Omnibus Reconciliation Act of 1990
   c. Orphan Drug Act of 1983
   d. Kefauver-Harris Amendment

   This item was published in the Test Bank for *Pharmacology*, 2nd ed., Fulcher, Fulcher, and Soto, Chapter 1: Legal and Ethical Aspects of Pharmacology, p. 4. Copyright Elsevier (2009).

4. Drug standards are the same in all states and countries. True/False

   This item was published in the Test Bank for *Pharmacology*, 2nd ed., Fulcher, Fulcher, and Soto, Chapter 1: Legal and Ethical Aspects of Pharmacology, p. 6. Copyright Elsevier (2009).

5. OTC drugs are not regulated by the FDA. True/False

   This item was published in the Test Bank for *Pharmacology*, 2nd ed., Fulcher, Fulcher, and Soto, Chapter 1: Legal and Ethical Aspects of Pharmacology, p. 6. Copyright Elsevier (2009).

6.  All drugs with the potential for abuse, as found under the auspices of the Controlled Substances Act of 1970, are followed by the DEA from manufacture to sale in a pharmacy or use by the physician. <u>True</u>/False

> This item was published in the Test Bank for *Pharmacology*, 2nd ed., Fulcher, Fulcher, and Soto, Chapter 1: Legal and Ethical Aspects of Pharmacology, p. 6. Copyright Elsevier (2009).

7.  Drug dependence is always unethical. True/<u>False</u>

> This item was published in the Test Bank for *Pharmacology*, 2nd ed., Fulcher, Fulcher, and Soto, Chapter 1: Legal and Ethical Aspects of Pharmacology, p. 8. Copyright Elsevier (2009).

8.  Prescription pads make wonderful notepads and paper for ordering blood tests and x-rays. True/<u>False</u>

> This item was published in the Test Bank for *Pharmacology*, 2nd ed., Fulcher, Fulcher, and Soto, Chapter 1: Legal and Ethical Aspects of Pharmacology, p. 9. Copyright Elsevier (2009).

## Physical Therapy

9.  Which of the following would be outside the physical therapist's scope of practice?
    A.  Fitting a client with crutches
    B.  Joint mobilizations
    C.  Ergonomic assessment
    <u>D.</u>  Suggesting a client double her dosage of blood pressure medication

> This item was published in the Test Bank for *Introduction to Physical Therapy*, 4th ed., Pagliarulo, Chapter 1: The Profession of Physical Therapy, p. 2. Copyright Elsevier (2012).

10. What was the year of the first National Organization Meeting for early physical therapists?
    A.  1894
    B.  1911
    <u>C.</u>  1921
    D.  1932

> This item was published in the Test Bank for *Introduction to Physical Therapy*, 4th ed., Pagliarulo, Chapter 1: The Profession of Physical Therapy, p. 4. Copyright Elsevier (2012).

11. What year were men first admitted to the American Physiotherapy Association?
    A. 1920
    B. 1921
    C. 1922
    D. 1923

> This item was published in the Test Bank for *Introduction to Physical Therapy*, 4th ed., Pagliarulo, Chapter 1: The Profession of Physical Therapy, p. 4. Copyright Elsevier (2012).

### Psychiatric Nursing

12. In 1952, Hildegard Peplau defined the psychiatric nurse's role as:
    1. a professional who helps patients with attitude adjustment needs.
    2. a nurse who is extensively trained to care for psychiatric patients.
    3. a resource person, a teacher, a leader, and a counselor to patients.
    4. a nurturer, a provider of psychiatric care, and a leader in nursing.

> This item was published in the Test Bank for *Principles and Practice of Psychiatric Nursing*, 9th ed., Stuart, Chapter 1: Roles and Functions of Psychiatric-Mental Health Nurses: Competent Caring, p. 1. Copyright Elsevier (2008).

13. The contribution of Linda Richards that remains a part of contemporary psychiatric nursing practice is the idea that:
    1. psychiatric nurses should have advanced preparation.
    2. nurses should assess both the physical and the emotional needs of patients.
    3. psychotic behavior must be controlled before serious psychotherapy begins.
    4. basic physical needs must always be met before emotional needs are addressed.

> This item was published in the Test Bank for *Principles and Practice of Psychiatric Nursing*, 9th ed., Stuart, Chapter 1: Roles and Functions of Psychiatric-Mental Health Nurses: Competent Caring, p. 1. Copyright Elsevier (2008).

14. Hildegard Peplau's classic article "Interpersonal Techniques: The Crux of Psychiatric Nursing" directed psychiatric nursing's future growth by stating that the primary role of the psychiatric nurse was that of:
    1. leader.
    2. teacher.
    3. counselor.
    4. surrogate parent.

> This item was published in the Test Bank for *Principles and Practice of Psychiatric Nursing*, 9th ed., Stuart, Chapter 1: Roles and Functions of Psychiatric-Mental Health Nurses: Competent Caring, p. 2. Copyright Elsevier (2008).

15. During orientation to the inpatient psychiatric unit, new staff members are told, "Address all patients by their title and surname, for example, Ms. Jones or Mr. Rodriguez, until you are directed by the patient to do otherwise." The philosophical belief underlying this directive is the idea that:
    1. every individual has the potential to change.
    2. the individual has intrinsic worth and dignity, and each person is worthy of respect.
    3. the goals of the individual are growth, health, autonomy, and self-actualization.
    4. the person functions as a holistic being who acts on, interacts with, and reacts to the environment as a whole person.

    > This item was published in the Test Bank for *Principles and Practice of Psychiatric Nursing*, 9th ed., Stuart, Chapter 1: Roles and Functions of Psychiatric-Mental Health Nurses: Competent Caring, p. 3. Copyright Elsevier (2008).

16. A psychiatric aide says, "I don't know why that patient does all that silly giggling and posturing. It's senseless!" The best reply to this comment would make reference to the psychiatric nursing principle that states:
    1. every individual has the potential to change.
    2. illness can be a growth-producing experience for the individual.
    3. all behavior is meaningful, arising from personal needs and goals that can be understood only by the person performing the behavior and within the context in which it occurs.
    4. the individual has the right to self-determination, including the decision to pursue health or illness through participation in the decision-making process regarding both physical and mental health.

    > This item was published in the Test Bank for *Principles and Practice of Psychiatric Nursing*, 9th ed., Stuart, Chapter 1: Roles and Functions of Psychiatric-Mental Health Nurses: Competent Caring, p. 4. Copyright Elsevier (2008).

17. The role of the psychiatric nurse in today's contemporary practice settings is:
    1. centered on the nurse-patient partnership.
    2. concentrated on psychosomatic therapies.
    3. centered on management of the patient's daily needs.
    4. caring for chronically ill psychiatric patients in acute-care settings.

    > This item was published in the Test Bank for *Principles and Practice of Psychiatric Nursing*, 9th ed., Stuart, Chapter 1: Roles and Functions of Psychiatric-Mental Health Nurses: Competent Caring, p. 4. Copyright Elsevier (2008).

18. Clinical rotations for nursing students include a psychiatric mental health rotation to give the student an opportunity to:
    1.  become familiar with patients who have chronic psychiatric mental health issues.
    2.  work with patients who have psychiatric as well as physical health issues.
    3.  learn to work with patients with various psychiatric mental health issues.
    4.  learn to care for patients who have emotional disorders.

    > This item was published in the Test Bank for *Principles and Practice of Psychiatric Nursing*, 9th ed., Stuart, Chapter 1: Roles and Functions of Psychiatric-Mental Health Nurses: Competent Caring, p. 4. Copyright Elsevier (2008).

19. We need to advocate the funding of outcome studies because they:
    1.  increase patient compliance with therapeutic regimens.
    2.  document quality, cost, and effectiveness of psychiatric nursing.
    3.  update psychiatric nursing specialists on new practice developments.
    4.  lead to the implementation of untried interventions and practice guidelines.

    > This item was published in the Test Bank for *Principles and Practice of Psychiatric Nursing*, 9th ed., Stuart, Chapter 1: Roles and Functions of Psychiatric-Mental Health Nurses: Competent Caring, p. 6. Copyright Elsevier (2008).

20. In the 1960s the psychiatric nurse began to shift to primary prevention and psychiatric nursing practice began to focus more on community care. This focus was initiated by which act?
    1.  The Primary Prevention Act of 1960
    2.  The Deinstitutionalization Act of 1961
    3.  The Therapeutic Community Act of 1962
    4.  The Community Mental Health Centers Act of 1963

    > This item was published in the Test Bank for *Principles and Practice of Psychiatric Nursing*, 9th ed., Stuart, Chapter 1: Roles and Functions of Psychiatric-Mental Health Nurses: Competent Caring, p. 8. Copyright Elsevier (2008).

*Dental Hygiene*

21. Another name for geographic tongue is:
    a.  median rhomboid glossitis.
    b.  benign migratory glossitis.
    c.  fissured tongue.
    d.  black hairy tongue.

    > This item was published in the Test Bank for *Oral Pathology for the Dental Hygienist*, 5th ed., Ibsen and Phelan, Chapter 1: Introduction to Preliminary Diagnosis of Oral Lesions, p. 2. Copyright Elsevier (2009).

22. When antifungal therapy is used to treat angular cheilitis, which diagnostic process is being applied?
    a.  Microscopic
    b.  Laboratory
    c.  Surgical
    d.  Therapeutic

    > This item was published in the Test Bank for *Oral Pathology for the Dental Hygienist*, 5th ed., Ibsen and Phelan, Chapter 1: Introduction to Preliminary Diagnosis of Oral Lesions, p. 6. Copyright Elsevier (2009).

23. A lesion with a stemlike base is described as:
    a.  a sessile.
    b.  a macule.
    c.  pedunculated.
    d.  a lobule.

    > This item was published in the Test Bank for *Oral Pathology for the Dental Hygienist*, 5th ed., Ibsen and Phelan, Chapter 1: Introduction to Preliminary Diagnosis of Oral Lesions, p. 7. Copyright Elsevier (2009).

## Statistics

1.  The relative frequency of a class is computed by:
    a.  dividing the frequency of the class by the number of classes
    b.  dividing the frequency of the class by the class width
    c.  dividing the frequency of the class by the total number of observations in the data set
    d.  subtracting the lower limit of the class from the upper limit and multiplying the difference by the number of classes
    e.  adding the lower limit of the class to the upper limit and multiplying the sum by the number of classes

    > From Mendenhall/Beaver/Beaver. *Introduction to Probability and Statistics*, 14E. © 2013 Brooks/Cole, a part of Cengage Learning, Inc. Reproduced by permission. www.cengage.com/permissions

2. Which of the following is not the goal of descriptive statistics?
   a. summarizing data
   b. displaying aspects of the collected data
   c. reporting numerical finding
   <u>d.</u> estimating characteristics of the population based on a sample
   e. none of these

3. Which of the following statements is correct?
   a. Univariate data results when a single variable is measured on a single experimental unit.
   b. Bivariate data result when two variables are measured on a single experimental unit.
   c. Multivariate data result when more than two variables are measured.
   <u>d.</u> All of these statements are true.
   e. None of these statements is true.

4. The set of all possible observations about a specified characteristic of interest is:
   a. a frame
   b. a multinomial data set
   c. an observational study
   <u>d.</u> a population
   e. all of these

5. A market share of 78.5 percent would be represented in a pie chart by a slice with a central angle of:
   a. 78.5 degrees
   b. 39.3 degrees
   c. 282.6 degrees
   d. 141.3 degrees
   e. 157 degrees

6.  Ms. Jenkins believes that her class of gifted children is higher in intelligence than the average population IQ of 100 with a standard deviation of 15. The average IQ score of the children in her class is 117. What is the most appropriate statistic for Ms. Jenkins to use?
    A.  z test
    B.  single-sample *t* test
    C.  paired-sample *t* test
    D.  independent-samples *t* test

Source: proola.org

7.  What is the probability we reject the null hypothesis, given the null hypothesis is false?
    A.  Power
    B.  Type I error
    C.  Type II error
    D.  Sampling error

Source: proola.org

8.  A university professor is interested to see if the average salary of college lecturers is related to what field they are teaching. Specifically, he hypothesizes that the average salary in the natural sciences is higher than that of lecturers in the social sciences. This example best illustrates what type of hypothesis test?
    A.  Null hypothesis
    B.  One-tailed test
    C.  Two-tailed test
    D.  Non-directional test

Source: proola.org

9.  A teacher wants to see if sugar consumption has an influence on preschool children's activity levels. She randomly assigns the preschool children into two groups. For one group, each child receives 5 pieces of candy with their breakfast; for the other group, the children do not receive any candy with their breakfast. After breakfast, the teacher records the children's activity levels and compares the two groups. The teacher finds that children who eat candies with their breakfast have higher activity levels than those who do not. What decision does this finding support?
    A.  Reject the null hypothesis
    B.  Fail to reject the null hypothesis
    C.  Accept the null hypothesis

Source: proola.org

10. The distribution for a statistics class has an average of 30, a median of 30, and a mode of 30. Which type of distribution does this represent?
   A.  Bimodal distribution
   B.  Normal distribution
   C.  Positively-skewed distribution
   D.  Leptokurtic distribution

11. Dr. Smith has a null hypothesis with a significance level of 0.12. In the population, the null hypothesis should be rejected. What type of error is Dr. Smith risking?
   A.  Type I Error
   B.  Type II Error
   C.  Sampling Error
   D.  Standard Error

12. Dr. Strange measures aggressive behaviors based on the number of times a student hits another student. What type of measurement scale is used to measure aggressive behavior?
   A.  Nominal
   B.  Ordinal
   C.  Interval
   D.  Ratio

13. A researcher uses a measurement scale to review survey scores. The scores are measurable, have a particular order, and are equidistant from each other. However, the scale lacks a meaningful zero. Which scale best describes this scenario?
   A.  Interval Scale
   B.  Ordered Scale
   C.  Ratio Scale
   D.  Nominal Scale

14. In statistics, measurement scales are grouped into four different types of scales: Nominal Scale, Ordinal Scale, Interval Scale, and Ratio Scale. Which of the following responses below would best fit the type of statistical analysis a researcher could perform if they were to use an Interval Scale?
    A. Percentiles
    B. Coefficient of Variation
    C. Standard Deviation
    D. Contingency Correlation

    Source: proola.org

15. Measurement involves the assignment of values to objects according to certain rules. The rules that guide the measurement process determine the type of measurement scale. Measurement scales are grouped into four different types including nominal, ordinal, interval, and ratio scales. Regarding different measurement scales, identify the correct statement(s) below.
    A. Non-parametric statistics and parametric statistics are permitted with nominal variables.
    B. Statistics permitted with ordinal variables include the median, mean, and any statistics based on percentiles.
    C. The ratio scale is an interval scale with a meaningful absolute zero, or a point at which there is an absence of the variable measured.
    D. In representing a variable, the further from a nominal scale the better, as once the scale is designated it cannot be downgraded into any of the scales below it.

    Source: proola.org

16. A student is gathering data on the driving experiences of other college students. One variable to be measured is the number of automobile accidents each student had during the previous year. What type of variable is this?
    A. discrete variable
    B. continuous variable
    C. categorical variable
    D. nominal variable

    Source: proola.org

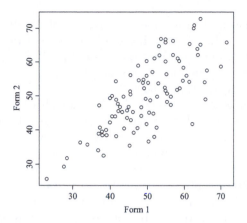

17. The scatterplot contains total scores from two forms of a test having a correlation of .60. How would the correlation be expected to change if it were calculated using only scores above 40 on both forms?
    A. Increase
    B. Decrease
    C. No change

Source: proola.org

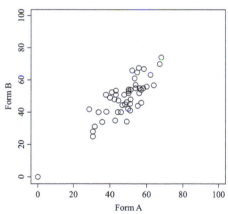

18. The scatterplot contains total scores from the two parallel forms (A and B) of a test. A group of 5 students scored zero on both forms. How would the parallel-forms reliability estimate change if these 5 students were removed from the calculation?
    A. Increase
    B. No change
    C. Decrease

Source: proola.org

*Matching Items*

19. What is the level of measurement for the variables in the following study? In the blank to the left of each variable, write the letter associated with the level of measurement that is employed (a–d). You may use a given type once, more than once, or not at all.

    Consider the following study:

    A program evaluator was asked to help a high school create a system to identify students who are likely to drop out of school. The variables that were significant include those listed below. These included the number of hours of TV or internet (online) viewing per day (the strongest indicator); reading scores (students who dropped out all had scores lower than the 50th percentile); whether the student failed a class during high school was a strong predictor. Oddly, grade-point average (0–4 point scale) had no association with dropping out and was never mentioned as a reason why students dropped out. There was also no association between dropping out and instructional methods students were exposed to. For each of these variables, indicate the level of measurement.

| Variable | Level of measurement |
|---|---|
| d  Amount of TV viewing | a. Nominal |
| a  Types of instructional methods | b. Ordinal |
| a  Whether a student drops out of school | c. Interval |
| c  High school grades | d. Ratio |
| a  Reasons given why they drop out | |
| b  Reading scores on the percentile scale | |
| a  Failed at least one class | |

Source: Authors

# Sciences

### Biology

1. From which molecule do organisms receive instruction to reproduce and grow?
   a. ATP
   b. carbon
   c. hydrogen
   d. DNA
   e. elements

2.  The pancreas is an organ that regulates blood glucose levels. When glucose levels rise above normal, the pancreas releases insulin to lower blood glucose levels. This is an example of _____.
    a.  evolution
    b.  mutation
    c.  immunity
    d.  homeostasis
    e.  variability

From Starr/McMillan. *Human Biology*, 11E. © 2016 Brooks/Cole, a part of Cengage Learning, Inc. Reproduced by permission. www.cengage.com/permissions

3.  In the following example of the hypothetico-deductive method, which item is the hypothesis?
    a.  What is the shape of the earth?
    b.  The shape of the earth may be round.
    c.  If so, can reach east by sailing west.
    d.  Columbus' voyage.
    e.  none of the above.

Reproduced with permission. Retrieved at http://courses. missouristate.edu/ChrisBarnhart/bio121/exams/prac1.pdf

4.  A mole of ethanol and a mole of hemoglobin (or any other molecule) will have an equal:
    a.  weight in daltons
    b.  mass in grams
    c.  number of atoms
    d.  number of molecules
    e.  volume

Reproduced with permission. Retrieved at http://courses. missouristate.edu/ChrisBarnhart/bio121/exams/prac1.pdf

5.  Which is not a property of water?
    a.  good solvent for electrolytes
    b.  high specific heat
    c.  adheres to polar compounds
    d.  contracts during freezing

Reproduced with permission. Retrieved at http://courses. missouristate.edu/ChrisBarnhart/bio121/exams/prac1.pdf

6.  The meaning of the symbol Σ is:
    a.  sum the set that follows.
    b.  multiply by the mean.
    c.  square root of the variance.
    d.  amphipathic.
    e.  Greek to me.

    Reproduced with permission. Retrieved at http://courses.
    missouristate.edu/ChrisBarnhart/bio121/exams/prac1.pdf

7.  The heat necessary to raise the temperature of a kilogram of water by
    1 degree Celsius is called a:
    a.  kilocalorie.
    b.  mole.
    c.  kilometer.
    d.  kilomole.

    Reproduced with permission. Retrieved at http://courses.
    missouristate.edu/ChrisBarnhart/bio121/exams/prac1.pdf

8.  Free energy is defined as:
    a.  heat.
    b.  entropy.
    c.  kinetic energy of molecules.
    d.  energy which does not cost anything.
    e.  energy which is available to do work.

    Reproduced with permission. Retrieved at http://courses.
    missouristate.edu/ChrisBarnhart/bio121/exams/prac1.pdf

9.  Which of the following structures is homologous to the wing of a bat?
    a.  The wing of a fly
    b.  The arm of a man
    c.  The eye of a newt
    d.  The tongue of an adder

    Reproduced with permission. http://courses.missouristate.edu/
    ChrisBarnhart/bio121/exams/prac4F10.pdf

10. Which of the following cannot evolve?
    a.  An individual
    b.  A population
    c.  A species
    d.  All of the above can evolve

    Reproduced with permission. http://courses.missouristate.edu/
    ChrisBarnhart/bio121/exams/prac4F10.pdf

11. The preservation of the sickle-cell form of hemoglobin in equatorial Africa, despite its deleterious effects is an example of:
    a.  natural selection.
    b.  artificial selection.
    c.  diversifying selection.
    <u>d</u>.  frequency-dependent selection.

12. The successive bases in a single DNA strand are held together by:
    a.  covalent bonds between phosphates.
    <u>b</u>.  covalent bonds between phosphate and deoxyribose.
    c.  covalent bonds between bases.
    d.  hydrogen bonds between phosphates.
    e.  hydrogen bonds between bases.

### Astronomy

13. The celestial object  _Pluto_  is just one of many small objects that orbit the Sun beyond Neptune.

14. The Universe is too big to discuss distance without using  _scientific notation_ .

### Physical Geography

15. Geography is often called the _____ science because it includes the recognition, analysis, and explanation of variations in phenomena as they are distributed on Earth's surface.
    a.  Earth
    b.  special
    <u>c</u>.  spatial
    d.  social

16. A condition or a process in one place generally has an impact on other places, this is known as:
    a.  spatial distribution.
    b.  a model.
    c.  spatial interaction.
    d.  spatial pattern.

From Petersen/Sack/Gabler. *Physical Geography*, 10E. © 2012
Brooks/Cole, a part of Cengage Learning, Inc. Reproduced
by permission. www.cengage.com/permissions

## Oceanography

17. Approximately what percent of the earth is covered by continents?
    a.  20
    b.  30
    c.  40
    d.  50
    e.  60

Source: Authors

18. Approximately what percent of the earth is covered by oceans?
    a.  40
    b.  50
    c.  60
    d.  70
    e.  80

Source: Authors

19. _____ can be extracted from seawater?
    a.  gold
    b.  silver
    c.  magnesium
    d.  amber

Source: Authors

20. The water cycle involves the exchange of energy leading to temperature changes. During which of the following processes within the water cycle do water molecules absorb energy?
    A.  Falling from the atmosphere
    B.  Evaporation from the ocean surface
    C.  Formation of ice from water
    D.  Formation of a cloud from water vapor

Source: proola.org

## Social Sciences

### *Adolescence*

1. Aristotle maintained that the key to adolescence is the development of
   A. the ability to be independent.
   B. the ability to engage in moral reasoning.
   C. the ability to choose.
   D. the ability to set goals.

   Source: Faculty

2. Which theorist postulated the focus on formal operational thought as a hallmark of adolescence?
   A. Piaget
   B. Erikson
   C. Freud
   D. Bandura

   Source: Faculty

3. Urie Bronfenbrenner was born in
   A. Pittsburgh, Pennsylvania.
   B. Ithaca, New York.
   C. Moscow, Russia.
   D. Saint Petersburg, Russia.

   Source: Faculty

4. Schools continue to explore partnerships with after-school programs, community agencies, and other youth-serving agencies. These partnerships are focusing on opportunities to promote youth involvement, providing for greater opportunities to explore interests, talents, and skills. Peter Benson and colleagues argue that these efforts are an important part of
   A. social cognitive learning.
   B. ecological learning.
   C. positive youth development.
   D. psychosocial development.

   Source: Faculty

5. The ecological model of youth development
   A. focuses attention on the role of communities.
   B. promotes youth appreciation of the environment.
   C. recognizes the many contexts in which youth exist.
   D. emphasizes the important roles of peers.

   Source: Faculty

6. Albert Bandura brought greater attention to the importance of social and environmental factors and their influence on behavior, whereas Erik Erikson drew attention to the internal struggles of identity formation. Bandura promoted the _____ theory of development, whereas Erickson promoted the _____ theory of development.
   A. social cognition; cognitive
   B. cultural; social cognitive
   C. social learning; psychosocial
   D. psychosocial; cultural

Source: Faculty

### Educational Psychology

7. The advantage of using the science of psychology to study human behavior is that
   a. most people give psychology lots of credibility.
   b. most teachers have a course in psychology and therefore understand it.
   c. psychology helps us to systematically notice and explain behavior.
   d. it is completely objective.

From Tuckman/Monetti. Educational Psychology, 1E.<br>© 2011 South-Western, a part of Cengage Learning, Inc.<br>Reproduced by permission. www.cengage.com/permissions

8. There are many behaviors and events going on in the classroom. This best describes the _____ of the classroom environment.
   a. immediacy            c. diversity
   b. multidimensionality   d. linearity

From Tuckman/Monetti. Educational Psychology, 1E.<br>© 2011 South-Western, a part of Cengage Learning, Inc.<br>Reproduced by permission. www.cengage.com/permissions

9. An ed psych student is eager for the class to start in the new semester. She is excited because she anticipates learning a formula for a successful teacher to apply in her classroom once she becomes a teacher. Will this student be disappointed and why?
   a. No—There are some specific principles that she can apply very easily to any classroom.
   b. No—There is a specific formula that guarantees success if applied to the classroom.
   c. Yes—The research indicates that no theory is correct.
   d. Yes—There are too many variables in teaching and learning for a formula for success. She will have to critically apply what she learns in ed psych to her own classes.

From Tuckman/Monetti. Educational Psychology, 1E.<br>© 2011 South-Western, a part of Cengage Learning, Inc.<br>Reproduced by permission. www.cengage.com/permissions

10. One of your friends says that learning in school reflects how we learn in real-life settings. Since you're taking an Educational Psychology course you disagree. Why?

    a.  Learning in school tends to be group-centered; learning in real-life tends to happen in an individualistic way.
    b̲.  Learning in school tends to be individualistic; learning in real-life tends to occur in groups.
    c.  Learning in school happens because of the teacher, but in real-life there is no teacher.
    d.  Learning in school tends to be temporary, but learning in real-life tends to be more permanent.

    From Tuckman/Monetti. *Educational Psychology*, 1E.
    © 2011 South-Western, a part of Cengage Learning, Inc.
    Reproduced by permission. www.cengage.com/permissions

11. If two different theories both do an adequate job of explaining behavior, the _____ theory is preferred due to _____.

    a̲.  simpler; parsimony              c.  newer; parsimony
    b.  simpler; transactional model     d.  newer; multidimensionality

    From Tuckman/Monetti. *Educational Psychology*, 1E.
    © 2011 South-Western, a part of Cengage Learning, Inc.
    Reproduced by permission. www.cengage.com/permissions

12. The correlation between time spent studying and grade is positive. What does that mean?

    a.  The relationship is beneficial for the student.
    b.  The two variables move in opposite directions.
    c̲.  The two variables move in the same direction; for example the more studying the higher the grades.
    d.  Research has found strong evidence for the correlation; a negative correlation would mean that there is weak evidence for the correlation.

    From Tuckman/Monetti. *Educational Psychology*, 1E.
    © 2011 South-Western, a part of Cengage Learning, Inc.
    Reproduced by permission. www.cengage.com/permissions

13. What should the correlation coefficient be between two variables to have practical value?

    a̲.  .00
    b.  .10
    c.  .40–.60
    d.  2.00–3.00

    From Tuckman/Monetti. *Educational Psychology*, 1E.
    © 2011 South-Western, a part of Cengage Learning, Inc.
    Reproduced by permission. www.cengage.com/permissions

14. What type of data is collected in observational/qualitative research in a classroom?
    a.  single-subject
    b.  correlational numerical data
    c.  baseline
    d̲.  Descriptive data that must be perceived and judged by the researcher.

From Tuckman/Monetti. *Educational Psychology*, 1E.
© 2011 South-Western, a part of Cengage Learning, Inc.
Reproduced by permission. www.cengage.com/permissions

15. Which of the following is the best example of why teachers need to appreciate diversity?
    a̲.  We live in a global, multicultural society
    b.  Not all of their students may speak English.
    c.  Students come from different social classes.
    d.  All of the above justify appreciation of diversity.

From Tuckman/Monetti. *Educational Psychology*, 1E.
© 2011 South-Western, a part of Cengage Learning, Inc.
Reproduced by permission. www.cengage.com/permissions

16. There is a perfect fit between the knowledge of educational psychology and its application to the classroom. True/F̲a̲l̲s̲e̲

From Tuckman/Monetti. *Educational Psychology*, 1E.
© 2011 South-Western, a part of Cengage Learning, Inc.
Reproduced by permission. www.cengage.com/permissions

### Psychology of Women

17. According to your text, a course in the psychology of women
    a̲.  explores psychological issues of specific concern to women.
    b.  demonstrates that women really are different from men.
    c.  illustrates that women from different ethnic groups are impressively similar to one another.
    d.  discovers evidence to show that women no longer experience gender discrimination.

From Matlin Margaret. *The Psychology of Women*, 7E.
© 2012 South-Western, a part of Cengage Learning, Inc.
Reproduced by permission. www.cengage.com/permissions

18. According to the information at the beginning of Chapter 1,
    a. women in countries such as Afghanistan are actually treated in a less biased fashion than women in the United States and Canada.
    b. topics such as pregnancy and rape are now a standard part of introductory psychology textbooks.
    c. psychologists have typically focused on men's experiences when they study topics such as achievement and retirement.
    d. women in the United States and Canada consistently earn higher salaries than men if we consider jobs that are traditionally female.

    From Matlin Margaret. *The Psychology of Women*, 7E.
    © 2012 South-Western, a part of Cengage Learning, Inc.
    Reproduced by permission. www.cengage.com/permissions

19. Which of the following students has the best understanding of the term "doing gender"?
    a. Alexei: "The phrase 'doing gender' refers to the process of conducting psychological research about gender comparisons."
    b. Irina: "The phrase 'doing gender' refers to a specific kind of historical analysis, which explores how women have been left out of the standard accounts of history."
    c. Sarah: "When people convey gender-related messages to each other—for instance, by the way they smile—they are 'doing gender.'"
    d. Peter: "When people work for gender equality—for instance, in the workplace—they are 'doing gender.'"

    From Matlin Margaret. *The Psychology of Women*, 7E.
    © 2012 South-Western, a part of Cengage Learning, Inc.
    Reproduced by permission. www.cengage.com/permissions

20. According to your textbook, the phrase "doing gender" means
    a. expressing our own gender, as well as responding to other people on the basis of their gender.
    b. conscientiously using the words sex and gender in an appropriate fashion.
    c. doing research that emphasizes gender similarities rather than gender differences.
    d. trying to be gender-fair in situations that would normally encourage gender-based discrimination.

    From Matlin Margaret. *The Psychology of Women*, 7E.
    © 2012 South-Western, a part of Cengage Learning, Inc.
    Reproduced by permission. www.cengage.com/permissions

21. Suppose that you are trying to explain the phrase "doing gender" to a high school student.
    Which of the following statements would be most accurate?
    a.    "Men are more likely than women to 'do gender.'"
    b.    "When a female student meets a male student, she may smile and act very interested in him; this is an example of 'doing gender.'"
    c.    "'Doing gender' is a phrase that applies to our perception of other people, rather than how we ourselves act."
    d.    "The ability to 'do gender' is programmed into our genetic makeup, and our culture has little influence on the way we 'do gender.'"

From Matlin Margaret. *The Psychology of Women*, 7E.
© 2012 South-Western, a part of Cengage Learning, Inc.
Reproduced by permission. www.cengage.com/permissions

22. According to the definition given in your textbook,
    a.    a feminist is someone who believes that women should have privileges that are denied to men.
    b.    men cannot be feminists.
    c.    a feminist has a high regard for women and believes that both genders should be treated similarly.
    d.    the research shows that people who refuse to call themselves feminists are highly unlikely to believe in the principles of feminism.

From Matlin Margaret. *The Psychology of Women*, 7E.
© 2012 South-Western, a part of Cengage Learning, Inc.
Reproduced by permission. www.cengage.com/permissions

23. During the 1970s,
    a.    books on the psychology of women were actually less available than they had been in the 1960s.
    b.    researchers began to investigate many new questions about the psychology of women.
    c.    researchers realized that the issue of gender was really much more straightforward than they had previously realized.
    d.    most psychologists realized that women had difficulties because their situations were at fault.

From Matlin Margaret. *The Psychology of Women*, 7E.
© 2012 South-Western, a part of Cengage Learning, Inc.
Reproduced by permission. www.cengage.com/permissions

24. According to your textbook's discussion of women of color,
    <u>a.</u>　the United States currently has more Latina/o residents than Black residents.
    b.　people who have recently immigrated to the United States from South America usually prefer to be called *Chicanas* or *Chicanos*.
    c.　most Black people in the United States report that they have never experienced racism.
    d.　because Asian Americans are considered the "ideal minority group," they seldom experience stereotyping based on their ethnic group.

    From Matlin Margaret. *The Psychology of Women*, 7E.
    © 2012 South-Western, a part of Cengage Learning, Inc.
    Reproduced by permission. www.cengage.com/permissions

### Learning and Behavior

25. Examples of behaviors that can be classically conditioned include
    a)　anxiety.
    b)　salivation.
    c)　blinking.
    <u>d)</u>　all of these

    From Powell/Honey/Symbaluk. *Introduction to Learning and Behavior*,
    4E. © 2013 South-Western, a part of Cengage Learning, Inc.
    Reproduced by permission. www.cengage.com/permissions

26. Judit is asked to report her precise thought patterns as she plans her next move in chess. This is an example of the method of
    a)　cognitive perception.
    b)　attentive perception.
    c)　cognitive elucidation.
    <u>d)</u>　introspection.

    From Powell/Honey/Symbaluk. *Introduction to Learning and Behavior*,
    4E. © 2013 South-Western, a part of Cengage Learning, Inc.
    Reproduced by permission. www.cengage.com/permissions

27. Which school of behaviorism is most likely to consider reports about thoughts and feelings to be unscientific?
    a) radical behaviorism
    <u>b)</u> methodological behaviorism
    c) neobehaviorism
    d) social learning theory

    From Powell/Honey/Symbaluk. *Introduction to Learning and Behavior*,
    4E. © 2013 South-Western, a part of Cengage Learning, Inc.
    Reproduced by permission. www.cengage.com/permissions

28. Behaviorists _____ the role of genetic factors in learning.
    a) have a growing appreciation for
    b) reject
    c) ignore
    d) focus upon

> From Powell/Honey/Symbaluk. *Introduction to Learning and Behavior,*
> 4E. © 2013 South-Western, a part of Cengage Learning, Inc.
> Reproduced by permission. www.cengage.com/permissions

### Education

29. Ms. Olive received advanced training in measurement and assessment and is a coach who provides assessment training to mathematics teachers in her school district. Many teachers come to her with questions on how to best assess their students in mathematics.

    A high school Algebra teacher asks Ms. Olive about the optimal assessment for measuring students' understanding of factoring. Which of the following methods is most appropriate in this situation?
    A. Selected response methods
    B. True/false statements
    C. Essay prompts
    D. Computation problems

> Source: proola.org

30. A teacher is asked to identify students who could benefit from interventions due to academic and/or behavioral struggles. Scores from which of the following assessments could help the teacher identify struggling students?
    A. Formative Assessments
    B. Summative Assessments
    C. Performance Assessments
    D. All of the above

> Source: proola.org

31. The Wechsler Individual Achievement Test measures a person's academic ability in four areas: Math, Reading, Written Language, and Oral Language. Based on the results, a teacher would know if a student's ability is at or below the level of their peers. This measurement indicates that the WIAT is
    A. norm-reference
    B. criterion reference

> Source: proola.org

32. Which option below is an example of a classroom management technique that uses negative reinforcement?
    A. A teacher gives a student a sticker for turning homework in on time.
    B. A teacher tells a student they did a good job for helping a friend.
    C. A teacher smiles at the class for following directions.
    <u>D</u>. A teacher says homework will be optional if everyone works together.
    Source: proola.org

33. A student has earned a score at the 75th percentile in the state. What is the correct interpretation of this result?
    <u>A</u>. That 25% of the students in the state earned a higher score on the examination.
    B. The student correctly responded to 75% of the items on the examination.
    C. The student scored in the top 25% of the students in the school who took the examination.
    Source: proola.org

34. You and a colleague are conducting a student observation to determine the amount of time a particular student spends off-task during a math period. How would you interpret a correlation coefficient of .55 between your rating and your colleague's rating?
    A. There is a weak positive relationship
    B. There is no linear relationship
    C. There is a strong positive relationship
    <u>D</u>. There is a moderate positive relationship
    Source: proola.org

## *Psychology*

35. Think-aloud procedures
    <u>A</u>. may occur during or after a prompt.
    B. occur after a prompt.
    C. occur before a prompt.
    Source: proola.org

36. Social psychology does NOT focus attention on which of the following?
    A. the study of the nature of individual behavior in group situations
    B. the study of the causes of individual behavior in group situations
    C. the study of the influence of other people on human behavior
    <u>D</u>. the study of intra-individual psychological states
    Source: Authors

37. Which of the following criticisms can be applied to social-cognitive theory?
    A. Learning is not recognized as a source of individual differences.
    B. It fails to account for maturation throughout the lifespan.
    C. It does not address the role of observing others in learning.
    D. It ignores the influence of the environment.

    Source: Authors

38. A positive psychology orientation argues that only way to help people reach their potential is through a focus on positive states, such as optimism and well-being. True/False

    Source: Authors

39. Participant observation and other qualitative methods are not only important tools to study constructs that are difficult to operationalize or measure, they are critical to explore concepts with people who may not have ready-made answers. True/False

    Source: Authors

## Example Item Reviews

What follows is a careful review of the example items presented earlier. The review was closely aligned to the item-writing guidelines presented in Chapter 4. We must emphasize that these items were gathered for the purpose of demonstrating how difficult it is to write items that are consistent with the item-writing guidelines. Expert item writers recognize that item writing is a collaborative process and depend on strong editing and item review procedures to ensure their efforts are maximized.

This is a real challenge for college instructors. We typically don't have access to editors who can review our test items before we administer them. But we do have colleagues, and a valuable routine would be to develop a culture of assessment literacy in a department or college to improve testing and assessment practices—all in the spirit of improving teaching and learning.

The reviews that follow are presented in the same order as the items are listed. Each item subject area and item number are followed by one or more item-writing guideline numbers presented in Chapter 4. We also recognize that there may be other guidelines that could be applied to any given item, improving it even further.

## Business

### *Managing Quality*

1. Guideline: 1. Items that contain the word "and" often introduce multiple aspects of content. This complicates interpretation for the student (Which part do I respond to?) and for the instructor (Which part was misunderstood?).

2. Guideline: 1. Is the point to consider business failures or stock price drops? Does the answer fit equally for both conditions?
3. Guideline: 22b. The presence of specific terms, in this case "solely," indicates that the item is unlikely to be true.
4. Guidelines: 4. This is likely relatively unimportant content; perhaps a theme or information from the book is more important than its author.
   7. The book has already been written, so "is" should be replaced with "was."
   17. Options should be alphabetically ordered.

### Human Resource Management

5. Guideline: 12. The word "not" in the stem should be stressed by bolding it in all capital letters.
6. Guidelines: 11. The main idea is not in the stem, only the subject. Because of this, the item requires a lot of reading.
   9. Each option contains multiple components, creating a lengthy item for a single point of information.
7. Guideline: 10. The format of the stem should be a complete question or a statement that is completed in the options—the blank should occur at the end of the statement, not the beginning.
8. Guideline: 7. The word "is" should be "are" since it refers to both values and beliefs (plural).
9. Guidelines: 12. The stem should be worded positively—eliminating the word "false." At least it's emphasized in all caps.
   21. In addition, the options should be worded positively; since b is negatively worded, it presents a double-negative. This would be more informative as a multiple true-false item.
10. Guidelines: 19. Since we are not content experts, we caution the use of options like these, where profitability is a function of cost and revenue, where all three are often interconnected and overlap.
    22f. Options are not homogenous, where option d is substantively different than the others.

### Business Research

11. Guidelines: 4. This may not be important content, as it is simply asking for an explanation of the acronym RFP.
    22c. There are multiple forms of clang associations, since multiple words in the stem are contained in the options.
12. Guidelines: 20. Avoid "all of the above."
    22c. There is a clang association in the use of "effective," as it appears both in the stem and option B.
13. Guideline: 22c. There is a clang association in the use of "sampling," since it appears in the stem and "samples" appears in the correct option C.

14. Guidelines: 7. Option B needs to be edited so that it reads "Business research supports" rather than "support."
    11. The main idea is not in the stem. Can anyone even imagine what this test question is about from the stem? Without it containing the main idea, it is much easier for students to defend multiple correct options.
    21. The options should be worded positively. Since "cannot" is not emphasized in some way, it may be overlooked.
15. Guidelines: 10. The format of the question is neither a question nor a statement being completed by the stems. There is no instruction as to how the student is supposed to select an option.
    22e. The final option D is absurd, since the point of a course on business research is to learn about its importance and necessity.

## Health Sciences

### *Pharmacology*

1.  Guideline: 15. Distractor plausibility is uncertain in these options—at least to the extent that they are not homogenous (related to Guideline 22f that options should be homogenous in content).
2.  Guidelines: 17. Since these options are proper titles, they should be in alphabetical order.
    20. Avoid using "all of the above."
    22e. Even a novice pharmacology student should recognize that the "Bureau of Dangerous Drugs" is absurd.
3.  Guidelines: 15. Even novice pharmacology students should recognize that the "Orphan Drug Act" is not plausible.
    17. Since these options are proper titles, they should be in alphabetical order.
4.  Guideline: 22b. The use of specific determiners, such as "all," makes this claim unlikely to be true.
5.  Guideline: 12. The use of "not" should be avoided, or it should be emphasized so that it is not overlooked. But remember, negatively wording the statement in true/false items creates a cognitively complex task in a way that may be unrelated to the purpose of the test.
6.  Guideline: 9. Minimize the amount of reading. Here it is unclear whether the point of the item is in recognizing the kinds of drugs at issue, understanding the role of the Controlled Substances Act, knowing that the act was passed in 1970, or acknowledging the condition under which controlled substances are handled.
7.  Guideline: 22b. The use of specific determiners, such as "always," makes this item unlikely to be true.
8.  Guideline: 22e. Even the most novice pharmacology student should recognize the ridiculous assertion in this item. Be wary of the use of humor in tests, but feel free to consider it if it is consistent with the course and lecture style and is not used on high-stakes exams.

*Physical Therapy*

9. Guidelines: 22a. The correct option, D, is much longer than any other option—a very common error among classroom instructors.

    22f. The options are not homogenous; some start with a verb, and others do not.

10. Guidelines: 2. This is likely a simple recall item based on material directly from the textbook or lecture notes rather than using new material to test higher-order skills.

    4. There are likely more important concepts regarding the origins of the physical therapist professional organization than the date.

11. Guidelines: 2. This is a simple statement, likely from the textbook or lecture notes.

    4. This item taps a very specific element of content that is not likely to be a core concept in the study of physical therapy.


*Psychiatric Nursing*

12. Guidelines: 22c. This item contains a clang association, since "nurse" appears in both the stem and the options 2 and 4, both of which are not correct.

    7. A minor editing point is in the use of a colon (:) in items where the options complete the stem. If this stem was written out as a complete sentence, the colon would not be used—since it is not the correct use of a colon. We should write the phrase and options so that they constitute a complete and accurately written sentence. This is true of questions 12 through 19 in this section.

13. Guidelines: 19. Options 2 and 4 contain common elements and may overlap. This is mostly a problem because the other two options do not contain these elements.

    22d. Because options 2 and 4 contain common elements, these could also be considered a pair, suggesting one is correct.

14. Guideline: 3. If this item was presented with questions 12 and 13, it overlaps with the content so that the answer to question 14 is known. Question 12 contains the definition of a psychiatric nurse's role, including options 1, 2, and 3 in Question 14.

15. Guidelines: 7 and 9. There is a lot of text and some redundancy in this item, including the problem that the first option is a single phrase whereas other options are multiple phrases.

    15. Not all of the options are plausible options to the directive regarding calling patients by their formal names. Options 1 and 4 are unrelated to personal regard.

16. Guidelines: 5. This item borders on an opinion issue, but the source of the opinion is unclear.

    22a. The options vary in length from 7 words to 29 words.

    22c. There is a form of a clang association in the use of the opposite terms of "senseless" and "meaningful," providing a clue to the correct option, 3.

17. Guideline: 19. The options overlap in that they all introduce multiple roles of a psychiatric nurse. The stem begins with "The role" as though there is only one role.
18. Guideline: 9. There is some redundancy in the stem and options, including extra wording that is unnecessary. The stem could be shortened by deleting the first seven words, while the second phrase can be rewritten accordingly.
19. Guideline: 9. The phrase "We need to advocate the funding of" is unnecessary to selecting the correct option.
20. Guidelines: 2. This item is a simple recall item that only requires students to identify the real act without knowing anything about its purpose or effect.
    15. The distractors should be plausible—health-related acts that are real rather than made up for the purpose of the test.

### Dental Hygiene

21. Guidelines: 22c. There is a clang association, since the word "tongue" appears in the stem and two options.
    22d. There are two pairs of options, one with "glossitis" and one with "tongue."
22. Guidelines: 7. There is a statement about a therapy being used, then a question about a diagnostic process being applied. These seem inconsistent.
    8  Regarding unnecessary content in the stem, the fact that the therapy is treating angular cheilitis is irrelevant to the question.
    22c. There is a clang association, since the word "therapy" is in the stem and the correct option is "therapeutic."
23. Guidelines: 7. Some editing is needed, since option b begins with a capital A.
    14. Here is an example where three options is sufficient, since the first three options are related to lesions (requiring some subject-matter knowledge to see this) and a lobule is a small lobe, not related to the others.

### Statistics

1. Guidelines: 22d. Three options start with "dividing the frequency of the class," presenting a triplet of options. All options should be structured the same.
   7. Edit and proof—this is a minor point, but part of good item writing. The stem is a statement that is completed by the options. So there should not be a colon at the end of the stem (it is not correct punctuation), and the options should end with a period to complete the sentence.

2. Guidelines: 9. The stem can be shortened by deleting "of the following." And option d can be shortened by deleting "based on a sample."

   12. The stem should be worded positively, or "not" should be emphasized.

   20. "None of these" should be eliminated as an option.

3. Guidelines: 11. There is no main idea in the stem. This would be better written as a multiple true-false question or a set of true-false questions.

   20. "All of these" and "None of these" should be eliminated. If the student knows two options are correct, they know the third option is also correct.

4. Guidelines: 15. Option c is not plausible, since a study is not a set of observations.

   16. Technically (as this is the area of our expertise), there may be multiple correct options. The set of all possible observations can be considered as the population or the "sampling frame," which is the list from which we draw the sample—the observable individuals from the population.

   20. Eliminate "all of these."

   22c. There is a clang association with the words containing "observation" in the stem and option c.

5. Guidelines: 8. Minimize language complexity by replacing the conditional tense "would be" with "can be."

   13. The repetition of "degrees" can be placed in the stem, for example: A market share of 78.5 percent can be represented in a pie chart by a slice with what degree angle?

   17. Options should be ordered numerically.

   22f. The options should be homogenous so that all values have one decimal (157.0).

6. Guidelines: 9. Minimize reading; the stem can be shortened.

   22d. The options present a triplet related to the $t$-tests, even though there are also different forms of $z$-tests that can be used to balance the options. A technical issue is the assumption in using the $z$-test, since using the $z$-test depends on knowing the population SD (but is the sample from the same population?).

7. Guidelines: 15. Option D is not plausible, since sampling error is not a probability.

   22f. Similarly, the options are not homogenous—since sampling error is not related to the null hypothesis.

8. Guidelines: 9. Minimize reading; the first two sentences can be combined and shortened.

   15. All options are not plausible—since option A (null hypothesis) is not a test.

   16. The correct option is not clear, since the hypothesis is not a test—the test is determined by which statistic is computed; he's stating the alternate hypothesis.

9. Guidelines: 9. Minimize reading; the stem can be reduced to less than half the current number of words.

    15. The options are not all plausible; we never accept the null hypothesis.

10. Guidelines: 16. There may be more than one correct answer, since a leptokurtic distribution can also have a mean, median, and mode in the same position; it's just more concentrated around the mean (greater kurtosis).

    13. The word "distribution" can be eliminated from each option, since it is referenced in the stem.

11. Guideline: 15. The distractors are not all plausible, since C and D are not the result of the null-hypothesis test. For most null-hypothesis statistical tests at this level, the standard error is based on sampling error. This should be an alternate-option MC item.

12. Guideline: 16. This may have multiple correct options. In and of itself, the number of times a student hits another student is a simple count on a ratio level of measurement. However, as an indicator of aggressive behavior, one hit may not equal another hit, as some hits may be more powerful and aggressive—indicating an ordinal level of measurement. The item writer has introduced an inadvertent complexity to the item by creating a more complex inference regarding aggression than the simple observation of hits.

13. Guidelines: 9. Minimize reading; the first sentence is unnecessary.

    17. The options should be in logical order, as done in question #12.

14. Guidelines: 8. The language complexity can be reduced by avoiding conditional tenses (would, could, were to); active voice is preferred (using "can" instead of "could").

    9.  Minimize reading; the first sentence is unnecessary, and "Which of the following responses below would best fit" can be reduced to "What is . . ."

    7.  Options should be in alphabetical order.

    16. There may be more than one correct answer; the coefficient of variation is a function of the SD and is similarly possible with an interval scale.

15. Guidelines: 9. Minimize reading; the first three sentences are not necessary. This item could be a set of true-false items, providing more information than the current item.

    22a. The options vary in length from 11 words to 29 words.

16. Guidelines: 9. Minimize reading; the first sentence is unnecessary, and the next two sentences can be combined into one.

    13. Eliminate repetition by deleting "variable" from each option—it's not necessary.

    22f. The options are not homogenous, since they are based on different typologies or types of variables.

17. Guidelines: 9. Minimize reading; the first sentence is unnecessary. In addition, the illustration is interesting but not needed to answer the question about the effect of range restriction.

    17. Option should be ordered logically ("no change" should be in the middle).

18. Guideline: 9. Minimize reading; the first sentence is unnecessary. In addition, the illustration is interesting, but it may be unnecessary (window dressing).

19. Guideline: None (that we can see)! This is a good example of a context-dependent set of matching items.

## Sciences

### Biology

1. Guidelines: 15. The distractors are not all plausible, since elements (e) are too encompassing.

    17. Options should be in alphabetical order.

    19. Options are not independent since carbon (b) and hydrogen (c) are elements (e).

2. Guidelines: 9. Minimize reading; the first sentence is unnecessary.

    17. Options should be in alphabetical order.

3. Guidelines: 15. All options may not be plausible, since a hypothesis is a claim, and option a is a question and option d is not a claim.

    20. Avoid "none of the above."

    22f. The options are not homogeneous in structure. Options c and d are not complete sentences.

4. Guidelines: 7. This item simply needs to be structured so that the option completes a sentence; delete the colon and add periods at the end of each option.

    9. The options contain unnecessary terms, including "in daltons" and "in grams." If weight or mass were the correct option, the unit wouldn't matter.

5. Guideline: 12. The stem should be worded positively; if needed, the negative word should be emphasized so that students don't overlook it.

6. Guidelines: 22e. Avoid humorous options, such as e.

    22f. The options are not all homogenous, since a and b are actions, c is a statistic, and d is an adjective describing a molecule.

7. Guidelines: 15. The options are not all plausible, since not all options are characteristics of heat.

    22d. There is a pair of options in b and d since both are quantities of moles.

8. Guideline: 22e. Avoid humorous options, such as d, which is a humorous reference to "free."

9.   Guidelines: 9. The stem could be shortened by deleting "of the fol-
     lowing." This is true in every item that begins with "Which of the
     following."

     22c. There is a clang association in the use of "wing" in both the stem
         and option a. Although this might be needed to include the same
         thing as a "wing of a bat" for students who have the misconception
         that homologous means the same structure on a different animal (or
         insect in this case).

10.  Guidelines: 12. The item should be positively worded; if necessary, the
     negative word "cannot" should be emphasized.

     19.  There is a pair of options in b and c that could be the same, since
         a population could be the entire species.

     20.  Avoid "all of the above."

11.  Guideline: 7. Every item deserves careful editing, where in this case,
     each option should end with a period.

12.  Guideline: 22d. The options present a triplet (a, b, and c) and a pair (d
     and e). Options d and e could be eliminated. Then "covalent bonds
     between" could be added to the stem.

### Astronomy

13.  Guidelines: 10. The stem for a short-answer item should be phrased so
     that the blank is at the end of the statement for maximum clarity.

     16.  There are other correct options, as suggested in the stem (one of
         many small objects), such as Haumea, Makemake, Eris, and many
         others. Either specify the type of object or be prepared for a large
         number of possible responses.

14.  Guideline: 16. Because the statement is so expansive, it is vague and
     ambiguous, with a large number of possible responses—not necessarily
     tied to a specific learning objective.

### Physical Geography

15.  Guidelines: 10. Item should be a phrase that is completed by the options
     with the blank at the end of the statement.

     15.  The distractors are not all plausible, since "special" is not a science
         (at least we don't think so).

     22c. There is a clang association, since "Earth" appears in the stem
         and the options. In addition, "special" and "spatial" are close in
         pronunciation, another form of clang association, which may
         present construct-irrelevant interference for nonnative English
         speakers.

16.  Guidelines: 7. Edit and proof—the stem is a run-on sentence.

     22d. There is a triplet in the options that includes the term "spatial,"
         setting it apart from the fourth.

### Oceanography

17. Guidelines: 3. If this item appears together with #18, it will create item dependence, since answering one essentially answers the other.
    15. If we can agree that it is common knowledge that the majority of the Earth is covered by oceans, then options of 50% or less are not plausible.
18. The relevant guideline is discussed above for item #17.
19. Guidelines: 10. The stem is not a statement to be completed by the options—the blank should appear at the end of the statement.
    15. The options may not all be plausible.
    17. The options should be in alphabetical order.
    22f. The options are not homogenous, since amber is not an element (the others are metals).
20. Guidelines: 22d. There is a pair of options beginning with "formation."
    9. Minimize reading; the first sentence is unnecessary.

## Social Sciences

### Adolescence

1. Guideline: 13. Avoid repetition, where "the ability to" can go in the stem.
2. Guidelines: 8. Minimize language complexity; the terms "postulated" and "hallmark" may be unnecessarily complex and could be replaced with "suggested" or "argued for" and "focus" or "major developmental step," respectively.
   17. Options should be ordered alphabetically.
3. Guidelines: 4. That may not qualify as important content.
   22d. There is a pair of options in that C and D both include Russia.
4. Guideline: 9. Minimize reading. There is a lot of context written into the stem that is unnecessary to correctly complete the main idea.
5. Guidelines: 11. Main idea is not in the stem, resulting in ambiguity.
   15. Option B may not be plausible, since appreciation of the environment is not part of youth development theories.
6. Guidelines: 1. Each item should focus on one topic or one task. This item should be divided into two different items.
   9. The first sentence is not needed to correctly respond to the item—which will help minimize reading.
   10. The options should complete the phrases, where the blank should be located at the end of each statement.

### Educational Psychology

7. Guideline: 22b. Avoid the use of specific terms, such as "completely." These are rarely correct.

8. Guidelines: 6. The options should be formatted vertically, not horizontally.

   10. The stem should be a statement that is completed by the options—with the blank at the end of the statement.

   15. "Linearity" is not a plausible option and is quite different than the others.

9. Guidelines: 1. The item is asking two different questions, one regarding disappointment and one regarding why. Each item should ask one question at a time.

   21. Options should be worded positively, where option c is negatively worded ("no theory").

   22a. The correct option is more than twice as long (30 words) as the next option length (14 words).

   22b. The use of specific terms, such as "guarantees," are rarely correct and provide a clue.

10. Guidelines: 10. This item appears to be an opinion question, which should be avoided, because of the use of language like "tends to be."

    13. There is repetition in the options that should be included in the stem ("Learning in school tends to be").

    22f. Options should be homogeneous; option c is currently phrased differently.

11. Guidelines: 1. The item should only tap one aspect of content, asking only one question instead of two.

    6. Options should be formatted vertically, not horizontally.

12. Guidelines: 8. Minimize language complexity by removing conditional tense of "would."

    14. This is a good example of an item that should have three options.

    22d. The two options including "two variables move in" present a pair that should be avoided.

    22a. The two last options are much longer than the first two, both including explanations that are unnecessary.

13. Guidelines: 7. Edit and proof—this item is incorrectly keyed, as the correct option cannot possibly be a and is most likely c.

    15. Not all distractors are plausible, since correlations cannot be larger than 1.0, as in option d.

    16. There are multiple correct options. Since we don't know what the variables are in this study, it is possible (although less likely) that a correlation of .10 can be of practical value for some purposes.

14. Guidelines: 7. Edit and proof—option d ends with a period, which is unnecessary since it is not a complete sentence.

    16. There may be multiple correct answers, since observational research can be used to establish a baseline and qualitative data can be single subject (especially in special education classrooms).

    22a. The correct option is more than three times longer (11 words) than the next longest option (3 words).

    22f. Options are not homogenous in structure or content.

15. Guidelines: 7. Edit and proof—the sentence for option a is missing a period.

    16. Although option a may be the best option, one could make the argument that all options are reasons. Because the question asks for the "best example," it appears to be an opinion-based item, or at least it depends on the context any given teacher faces.

    20. Avoid "all of the above." Specifically, option d (all of the above) is not an example of why teachers should appreciate diversity (although in this case it might be a correct option).

    21. Options should be worded positively; if option b must begin with "Not," it should be emphasized in some way.

16. Guideline: 22b. Avoid specific terms, such as "perfect," since these are rarely true.


## Psychology of Women

17. Guidelines: 11. The main idea is not in the stem, leading to ambiguity.

    21. The options should be positive, but option d employs the word "no" with no emphasis.

    22c. There is a clang association with the word "psychology," which appears in the stem and in the correct option.

18. Guidelines: 2. This item doesn't introduce or rely on new information but asks for identification of information from the textbook.

    11. The main idea is not in the stem—in fact, no ideas are presented in the stem. This set of options would be more informative to the course instructor if it were a set of true-false items.

19. Guideline: 9. The reading load can be minimized by reducing the reference to students and students' names—this is not necessary to answer the item correctly.

20. Guideline: 3. Notice that questions 19 through 21 are all about "doing gender." If more than one of these three items appeared in the same test, they would create item dependence, as answering one will provide a clue to answering the others.

21. Guideline: 9. The reading could be minimized by removing the reference to explaining the phrase to a high school student, which is not needed to answer the question. Even so, the options are not all in the context of high school student life.

22. Guidelines: 11. The main idea is not in the stem—again, the stem doesn't contain an idea. This would be better formatted as a set of true-false items.

    21 Options should be worded positively, or, if needed, the negative terms should be emphasized; for example "cannot" should be bolded and in all caps.

    22a. The options vary substantially in length from 4 to 21 words but should be more similar.

23. Guidelines: 11. The main idea is not in the stem, leading to ambiguity.
    15. The distractors don't all seem plausible, particularly option d, which
       is partially incomprehensible ("their situations were at fault").
24. Guidelines: 7. Edit and proof—there is no need for underlining certain
    terms in option b.
    11. The main idea is not in the stem, leading to ambiguity.
    21. Negative terms in the options (e.g., "never") should be emphasized
       (bold, all caps).

### Learning and Behavior

25. Guidelines: 15. The distractors are not all plausible, since anxiety is not
    a behavior.
    20. Avoid "all of the above."
26. Guideline: 22d. The options present two pairs, since two include "cogni-
    tive" and two include "perception."
27. Guidelines: 15. Social learning theory doesn't seem plausible, since it is
    not about internal thoughts or feelings.
    22c. There is a clang association in the first three options, since they
       include "behaviorism," which also appears in the stem.
    22f. The options are not homogenous in content or structure.
28. Guidelines: 10. The format is not a statement that is completed by the
    options—the blank should appear at the end of the statement or the
    stem should be rewritten as a complete question.
    22a. The correct option is more than twice as long as the next longest
       option.
    22f. The options are not homogenous in structure or content.

### Education

29. Guidelines: 9. Minimize reading by removing the first two sentences,
    which are unnecessary. The second two sentences can be shortened and
    combined.
    19. The options are not independent, since true/false items (option B)
       are a type of selected-response format (option A).
30. Guidelines: 9. Minimize reading by removing the first sentence, which
    is unnecessary.
    19. The options are not homogenous in content, since performance
       assessments can be used for formative or summative purposes. Forma-
       tive and summative are not types of assessment; they are different
       uses of assessments.
    20. Avoid "all of the above."
31. Guidelines: 7. Edit and proof—the correct form of the options should
    end in "referenced," and since the options complete the stem, they should
    end with a period.

9. Minimize reading by eliminating the first sentence, which is unnecessary, and combining the second and third sentences.

16. From this information alone, it is impossible to tell which option is correct, as both types of scores can be used to make an inference about the relative ranking of students.

32. Guidelines: 13. The words that are repeated in the options ("A teacher") can be added to the stem.

22f. The options are not homogenous in structure, since they end with a phrase using "for" (option A), "for" (B), "for" (C), and "if" (D), which makes the correct option different.

33. Guidelines: 22d. The options present a pair, where both begin with "The student."

22f. The options are not homogenous in structure since two refer to 25%—another option should be used to create balance, including reference to 75%.

34. Guidelines: 13. Remove the repetition in the options ("There is").

16. There may be more than one correct option. Since this is observational data, which likely results in moderate levels of reliability, and since lower reliability (more measurement error) reduces (attenuates) the magnitude of correlations, we could interpret a correlation of .55 as strong (it may not be possible to be any larger if the reliabilities are near the same magnitude).

17. The options should be in logical order.

### Psychology

35. Guidelines: 11. The main idea is not in the stem.

13. There is repetition in the options with the word "occur."

22d. There is a pair of options that simply uses "occur," whereas the first option is conditional and uses "may occur."

36. Guidelines: 12. The question should be written positively, avoiding NOT.

13. There is repetition in the options with "the study of."

22c. A clang association is present with the word "psychology" in the stem and "psychological" in the correct option.

22d. There is a pair of options regarding "individual behavior in group situations," potentially providing a clue that these are not correct.

37. Guidelines: 21. Two of the options contain "not," although each option is negatively phrased.

22f. Homogeneity is not present in the structure of the options, since three start with "it." The options could simply contain a list of things included (or not) in social-cognitive theory: learning as a source of individual differences, maturation throughout the lifetime, the role of observing others in learning, the influence of the environment.

38. Guidelines: 7. Editing should have caught a missing word in the statement: "argues that *the* only way . . . ."

    22b. The phrase "only way" is an extreme specific determiner that is rarely true.

39. Guidelines: 1. There are multiple ideas presented, in terms of being important tools, being difficult to operationalize and measure, and being critical to explore with a condition regarding people who may not have ready-made answers (a complex statement). There are possibly three separate items here.

    12. The phrase contains the negative word "not" in two different places, and they are not emphasized in any way.

# 7 Using Test Results to Improve Item Writing, Teaching, and Learning

All of our efforts in writing test items are intended to support the overarching goals of improving teaching and learning. Reviewing student item responses and evaluating test performance can also help us improve the item development process itself, both in terms of improving our ability to write effective items and in terms of improving features of individual items that we might use in the future. These improvements have the potential to inform instruction and learning.

In this chapter, we provide guidance to help you quickly review item responses and make decisions about the quality of individual items. The review process involves examining responses from the highest-performing students and then the frequencies with which incorrect options were selected or incorrect written responses were given. Taken together, this information can confirm that items are not flawed and can inform revising items for future use—as well as improving item-writing skills in general.

We end with a brief discussion on how test information can be used to inform instruction and learning.

## Chapter Learning Objectives

1. Identify three item analysis statistics (item difficulty, item discrimination, and distractor frequencies), and give details on how they are carried out and what information they each provide about item functioning.
2. Define reliability and explain its relevance to norm-referenced and criterion-referenced testing.
3. Explain, with examples, how analysis of item responses can be used to improve the item-writing process.
4. Summarize, with examples, how results from item and test analyses can be used formatively to improve learning.
5. Explain, with examples, how information from test and item performance can be used to improve instruction.

## How Can We Use Test Results to Improve Item-Writing and Test-Development Skills?

We can learn a great deal about our craft (testing) by evaluating the effectiveness and quality of our tests. There are many ways to collect quality information about our items and tests. Colleges and universities offer measurement services, including the scoring and evaluation of classroom tests. These include tests that can be offered online or using a machine-readable answer sheet, such as the infamous bubble answer sheet. Students respond on the bubble answer sheet or enter their answers online, and these data are analyzed by the measurement services office. The measurement services office then provides the instructor with an item analysis report.

Item analysis typically involves three factors, including item difficulty, item discrimination, and distractor frequencies. Test scores can also be analyzed in terms of their reliability. Each one of these analyses is briefly described here. It should be noted that the statistics used within these analyses are unstable with small samples. If your class has fewer than 30 students, then the only statistic that is worth worrying about is item difficulty—which is useful with any size of class. But item discrimination is often reported as a correlation (explained shortly), which can change dramatically by adding more responses—in a small class, even a single additional student can change a correlation from positive to negative. Similarly, distractor frequencies are most appropriate when there are many students, so we can see the response frequencies on all of the distractors. Finally, reliabilities are also very sensitive to sample size and to variability in student performance.

> For classes with fewer than 30 students, don't worry too much about test score analysis.

### Item Difficulty

Item difficulty is probably the most important information to the college instructor. Typically, this is reported as the proportion or percentage responding correctly to the item. In classical test theory, item difficulty for a dichotomously scored item (scored 0 or 1) is called the item $p$-value or proportion correct.

$$\text{Item difficulty} = \text{proportion correct} = \text{item } p\text{-value} = \frac{\# \text{ of Correct Responses}}{\text{Total } \# \text{ of Test Takers}}.$$

If 41 students answer the item correctly out of 50 students who took the test, that gives us an item $p$-value = 41/50 = .82. When the item has a $p$-value of .82, we know the proportion correct is .82, which is the same as saying 82% of the students answered the item correctly. Is this an easy item? The question about difficulty or easiness is relative. We addressed the ideas around item difficulty at the ends of Chapters 3 and 4 and say a bit more in what follows.

Novice item writers may equate item difficulty with cognitive level, but these are not the same. Knowledge items are not inherently or always easier than comprehension or application items. We can control MC item difficulty through the distractors. This is described in more detail in Chapter 4 (see item-writing guideline #15).

When test items allow for partially correct responses, particularly with CR items, the item difficulty is simply the average item score based on the total possible score for the items.

Item difficulty for partial-credit items = item mean =

$$\frac{Total\ \#\ of\ Points\ Obtained}{Maximum\ Score\ \times\ \#\ of\ Test\ Takers}.$$

We want item difficulty to be reasonable but also to reflect the natural challenge of the content. If our instruction is effective and students are learning, the item $p$-values should be high, as most students should get the items correct. When $p$-values are low, especially lower than .50, this indicates that students are not learning—and for whatever reason, it tells us that we need to revisit that content so as to prepare students for the next unit or the next course or for success in their chosen professions. This is particularly important when the content on our tests is prerequisite for successful learning of future content or future courses.

We can use item difficulty to determine what content needs more work. We can also use item difficulty to decide whether the items are functioning as intended. Sometimes items are very difficult or very easy for the wrong reasons—because of poor item writing. We definitely should pay attention to the most difficult items and possibly reconsider the easiest items to make sure they are free of clues and really do cover important content.

## Item Discrimination

Item discrimination measures the extent to which the item discriminates or differentiates students with low performance from those with high performance. If an item is measuring an important aspect of the total test, it should be serving like an indicator for the whole test. So if a student correctly responds to an item, they should be doing well on the test overall. If a student responds to an item incorrectly, they should be doing poorly on the test overall. This is why a correlation between the item and the total test is useful to us—incorrect item responses should indicate low test performance, and correct item responses should indicate high test performance.

We want item discrimination to be positive and ideally greater than .20. However, for classroom tests, particularly those with smaller samples, we should be satisfied with item discrimination values greater than 0. More effective items will produce higher positive discrimination values, indicating the items are strong contributors to the total score.

There are many forms of item discrimination. The most common forms are called item–total correlations, as they are based on correlations between the item score and the total score. But since the total score also includes the item score, it is best to correct the correlation so that the total score does not include the particular item for which we are computing the item discrimination value. These are typically called corrected item–total correlations or item–rest correlations (correlations between the item and the rest of the test). There are many versions of correlations that can be used to estimate the item discrimination values, where the most common are:

- Point-biserial correlation: a correlation between dichotomous scores (item score) and a continuous score (total test score). This is equivalent to the typical Pearson correlation. This is also affected by item difficulty, in that items that are very easy (nearly everyone gets right) or very difficult (nearly everyone gets wrong) will naturally have lower correlations, because there is very little variability in item scores. As an extreme example, if everyone gets the item right, the item–total correlation will be zero.
- Biserial correlation: a correlation between an artificially dichotomized score (assuming that there is a continuous score underneath the dichotomous one) and a continuous score. This often produces a higher value and is less affected by small samples and item difficulty.
- Polyserial correlation: similar to the biserial correlation, this correlation is appropriate for partial-credit items, where the item scores are more than 0 and 1.

Another way to measure item discrimination is through the D-index. This is the difference in the proportion correct of the higher-scoring and lower-scoring students. We expect that a larger portion of higher-scoring students and a smaller proportion of lower-scoring students will answer each item correctly, so the D-index should be positive (if it discriminates between upper- and lower-ability students). To calculate the D-index, we sort upper-scoring and lower-scoring students into groups. With small samples, this involves dividing the tests in two. If there are sufficient numbers, say, more than 100, we can take the upper 27% of tests and the lower 27% of tests based on total scores (there is some statistical optimality achieved with the upper and lower 27% of tests).

Item Discrimination = D-index =

$$\frac{\# \, in \, Upper \, Group - \# \, in \, Lower \, Group \, (asnwering \, item \, correctly)}{\# \, of \, Test \, Takers \, in \, a \, Group \, (or \, in \, the \, Larger \, Group)}.$$

Another way to estimate this is to take the proportion of the upper group having correct responses minus the proportion of the lower group having correct responses.

D-index = *Proportion Correct in Upper Group – Proportion Correct in Lower Group*

If .90 of the upper group answer correctly and .25 of the lower group answer correctly, that gives us a D-index = .90 – .25 = .65. This is a strong level of discrimination.

Overall, these measures tell us whether students who do well on the test also do well on the given item. If any of the values, the correlations or the D-index, are positive, this is a good result for our items. It suggests that the items do indeed differentiate among students of different abilities—that the items contribute meaningfully to the total test score.

When item discrimination values fall below zero, when they are negative, this indicates a problem with the item. It suggests that scores on the item are not consistent with total test scores overall. This means lower-ability students are equally or more likely to answer the item correctly than high-ability students (which shouldn't be possible). Some potential causes include:

1.  The item measures something different than the rest of the test, something not intended to be measured by the total test.
2.  The key is wrong and we have scored the item incorrectly. Either the wrong option was scored as correct or the item has more than one correct option.
3.  Students are not reading the item correctly or there is something in the item that is confusing students, particularly the high-ability students.
4.  There is a clue in the item that allows students to answer correctly, so it is unrelated to the total test score.

### Distractor Frequencies

A very important tool for the college instructor is found in the frequencies of responses to item distractors. Knowing which distractors students select tells us a great deal about what students hold as misconceptions, errors in thinking, problem-solving errors, and misinformation. When the distractors are carefully developed to represent misconceptions and common errors, they provide diagnostic information. Distractor analysis is the most important source of information for college instructors looking to find ways to better support student learning and to improve instructional practices (more on this in what follows).

The goal is to see at least some students selecting each distractor—but hopefully the lower-ability students (those with lower scores on the test overall). Ideally, distractors will be selected with equal frequency, as the goal is to make distractors equally plausible. But this is rarely achieved in practice.

Some measurement specialists have argued that we should expect to see at least 5% of the students select each distractor. But if the item is very easy, where most respond correctly, there may not be enough to select each distractor at 5%. If 90% of students answer the item correctly, then we hope to see the 10% spread evenly across the distractors. If 50% answer the item correctly, then we hope to see the remaining 50% spread evenly across the distractors. This is the ideal goal.

With small classes, particularly those with fewer than 30 students, we may not see every distractor selected in any particular class. We shouldn't overreact to distractors that are not selected in small classes. They may still be useful in the future.

We hope to see each distractor being selected by at least some students. For those distractors that are not selected, we may want to reconsider whether they are useful to us as distractors. Do they contain misconceptions or common errors? Are there other, more common misconceptions or errors that would be more effective distractors? The bottom line is that distractors that are not attracting any student responses should be reconsidered, possibly edited, or replaced. It is very difficult to create three or four effective distractors, which is why we recommend a total of three options for most MC items.

### Test Score Reliability

Test score reliability is a complex statistic. It basically tells us how consistent a test score might be. If we gave our students a different sample of items or wrote a different set of questions for the test, would they get the same scores? Reliability is a way to describe consistency over random or chance performance, and we care about consistency. But most test developers don't think too much about the basis of consistency. We know there are many different kinds of reliability, depending on how we define consistency. Do we care about consistency over different forms of a test with different items? Do we care about consistency over time? Do we care about consistency over contexts or testing conditions?

Internal consistency is the most common form of reliability, often estimated with coefficient alpha, the most frequently used index of test score reliability. Internal consistency lets us estimate the consistency of test scores based on the idea of sampling items from a larger domain of items. It essentially estimates sampling error based on the sampling of test items from an infinite pool of possible test items. It answers the question:

> How much variability in student test scores is due to true differences in ability versus sampling error due to sampling items?

We note that the typical form of reliability, coefficient alpha, is commonly incorrectly referred to as "Cronbach's alpha." Many refer to it as Cronbach's alpha because he wrote about it in 1951, but he did not introduce or derive the statistic we use as alpha; it was developed by a number of earlier researchers independently, including Guttman, Kuder, and Richardson. He named it coefficient alpha in an attempt to describe several characteristics of test score quality. However, he never returned to work on alpha or the other characteristics, as he turned his attention to Generalizability Theory (G-Theory), a much more flexible and meaningful model to evaluate test score quality. G-Theory is a way for us to estimate how much variance in test scores is due to different aspects (facets) of the measurement procedure. We can partition measurement error into different parts, like test items, occasions, and raters, in the event there is human scoring. This only makes sense in large-scale testing programs, but it's a useful way for us to think about the many aspects of a testing situation that can introduce measurement error. A good description of G-Theory compared to traditional reliability approaches is available by Brennan (2011), but this is grounded in a lot of measurement lingo. Another option to learn more about this approach is available in an example of using G-Theory to evaluate inter-rater reliability in agricultural education (VanLeeuwen, 1997). G-Theory is not typically applied to classroom tests.

Measures of internal consistency reliability are appropriate for norm-referenced tests, and most classroom tests are criterion referenced rather than norm referenced. Norm-referenced tests are designed to spread students out across the score scale, where scores depend on how other students perform. A norm-referenced score only tells us how the student performed compared to other students; it does not tell us what the student knows or can do. Norm-referenced tests include tests such as the ACT, SAT, GRE, and other admissions tests. These tests are specifically designed to spread students out as much as possible. They rank order students so we can identify the best among the test takers. In these kinds of tests, coefficient alpha tells us the extent to which the variability of student scores is due to their true abilities and not due to sampling error in the items. The more we spread students out, the more we are certain about their rank order, and the higher coefficient alpha will be.

Criterion-referenced tests are based on covering the content being tested; the scores can be referenced to what content was versus was not mastered by students. Examples of criterion-referenced tests include every state K–12 test measuring proficiency in reading, writing, mathematics, and science; most licensure and certification exams to ensure content and skill mastery; and nearly all classroom assessments that are intended to measure mastery of the instructional learning objectives. We don't necessarily care if students are spread out, and we don't just want to rank order students. We want to evaluate what students know and can do—to support the claims we hope to make about students—to evaluate the achievement of the instructional learning objectives. In many classes, many students will do well on some of the tests. But it is possible that all students do well. In any case, we find that variability on classroom tests is much less than what we might find on norm-referenced tests, resulting in lower estimates of internal consistency—lower reliability. This doesn't mean that classroom test scores are of lower quality or are less useful. Coefficient alpha and other estimates of internal consistency were not designed for criterion-referenced tests—classroom tests.

Do not use coefficient alpha to judge the quality of classroom tests.

## How Can We Use Test Results for Formative Purposes?

When we use test results to improve teaching and learning, we are explicitly engaging in formative uses of tests. Recall that in Chapter 1, we introduced the idea that test results can be used for formative or summative purposes. At least five features of assessments have been identified in the literature as being critical features of effective formative uses of assessment (McManus, 2008). These include:

1. Use learning progressions to clearly articulate key components of learning objectives. Learning progressions describe how students learn in a domain—how KSAs develop to support ongoing learning as students develop subject-matter expertise.
2. Clearly communicate to students the intended learning objectives and criteria for success. In order to achieve learning objectives, we must be clear about what the targets of learning are and provide examples of what success looks like.
3. Provide feedback that connects student performance to the learning objectives and criteria for success. Because of the importance of feedback, we discuss this more in what follows.
4. Promote self-assessment, encouraging students to think about their own learning. When the first three features are achieved, students are armed with tools to engage in self-evaluation of their own KSAs and can consider how their learning and studying behaviors are promoting success.
5. Create a classroom culture in which learning is seen as a partnership between the instructor and students. Learning can be enhanced through communities of learning and through cooperative learning (for many ideas on building cooperative learning activities in your course, see the *Cooperative Learning Newsletter*, which is available online at www.co-operation.org/journal-articles/). As instructors, we can model behaviors that create open and respectful environments in which students and instructors can share thoughts, concerns, and questions and share the responsibilities for learning.

## How Can We Use Test Results to Improve Learning?

Although we've mentioned this in a number of places, it is important to remember our mantra:

> *Students learn while preparing for the test, while taking the test, and while reviewing the test.*

We can begin to promote student learning by providing students with a clear and explicit set of course and instructional learning objectives. In addition, we need to provide our students with a copy of the test blueprint so they know the content and cognitive demands of the items and their relative emphasis. This provides students with full disclosure and awareness of the learning expectations and information about how their learning will be evaluated. We wrote earlier about the importance of opportunities to learn. When we provide the test blueprint, we are supporting that effort, as well as providing opportunities to perform. Students cannot prepare and perform to their optimal level if they don't know what to prepare for.

In our measurement classes, we involve the class in preparing the test blueprint for at least one test. In addition to teaching about the process of test blueprint development (an important objective in a measurement course), creating the test blueprint in class helps students understand how decisions are made in terms of what shows up on the test. This preempts concerns that the content balance is not right or that it wasn't clear what was going to be covered on the test.

A good exercise for students in any course is to ask them to write sample test questions. These can be used in preparation or review of an exam. It gives you an opportunity to practice your item-writing skills by critiquing the sample test items written by your students. It also helps students understand that item writing and test development are not easy tasks. Building assessment literacy among our students is always a positive unintentional consequence of practicing good test-preparation and test-administration activities in our classes.

If the test is well prepared, consistent with the test blueprint, and reflective of the instructional learning objectives (all of which was clearly communicated to students), it provides students with a concrete framework for understanding what is important in the subject matter—and in your course. When the test is well developed, it can communicate important organizational structures of content. It can help confirm students' understanding and the ways in which they have organized the materials in their minds. A well-developed test can help secure the storage of knowledge and skills in a useful way for students, further enhancing meta-cognitive skills (possibly an additional unintended consequence). Students reflecting on their abilities to respond to test items realize their strengths and weaknesses, or at least their confidence in understanding the material, and may engage in self-adjustment in the way they use and respond to the questions and the content of the questions. On the other hand, we also must recognize the inherent dangers here—if the test is poorly constructed, all of this potential learning from taking the test is turned into affirmation of misconceptions, disorganization of subject-matter content, and failure to realize one's own limited understanding.

> A poorly constructed test can do more damage than not testing at all.

More than any other activity, reviewing the results of a test is a great way to enhance student learning. This review should be more than a simple recitation of the correct answers. In your review of the test results, identify the items where students struggled the most (lowest percentage correct). Also, in those most challenging items, identify the distractors that attracted most students—and if these distractors were carefully constructed (as described earlier), you will have important information about the kinds of misconceptions or problem-solving or reasoning errors students still hold. These are the targets for intervention or additional instruction. These items can then be reworded for future tests to test student learning on previously poorly learned material. The conversations about test results should be based in the content of the course subject matter. And if possible, make yourself (or your TA) available to provide one-on-one review for students that may need additional supports.

## How Can We Use Test Results to Improve Instruction?

This might be the last section of the book, but it is not the least important. It goes hand in hand with using test scores to improve learning and support our claims about students and what they know and can do. A reflective instructor realizes that teaching and instruction matter. We make a difference. Think back on your own teachers throughout your life. You are sure to recall those that had an impact (hopefully many) and those that didn't (hopefully few). And although there is a great deal of controversy around the idea of using student test scores to evaluate teachers, there should be no question that student scores can be used to improve our instruction and assessment skills. There is no easier way to do that than learning how to reflect on the work and assessment results of our students in light of the instruction and learning opportunities we've provided.

There are two levels of test analysis that help us inform our teaching practices in terms of both evaluating prior teaching and planning for future teaching. These include reviewing the overall score distribution and performance at the item level.

### Overall Test Performance

How do students do on average? What is the range of scores? How well do most students do? These questions are about the score distribution or frequency of scores. We can create a simple tally of scores or enter them into a spreadsheet to create a histogram, representing the full distribution of scores. This also allows us to easily compute the average score.

We can also do this by grouping items into learning objectives if there are a small number of them on the test. The items within a specific learning objective can be summed together to get scores for each objective. This is useful only if there are multiple items per objective, at least five or so.

By reviewing total scores and, if possible, learning objective scores, we get a sense of the overall performance of students. However, there are two competing questions we may ask based on these results:

1. How well did students achieve the intended learning objectives?
2. Did my instruction and related activities provide students with opportunities to learn the intended learning objectives?

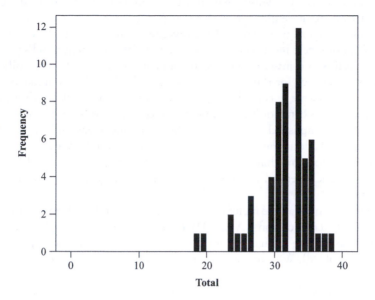

*Figure 7.1* Histogram of Test Scores for 56 Students

Histograms like these are generally not smooth because of smaller samples. There are many scores that are not observed—not obtained by the 56 students in this example. But it looks like students did fairly well on this 40-item test, although no students received perfect scores. In addition, a number of students achieved scores below 30 (75% correct), and a couple scored below 20 (50% correct). It is important to identify the items that may be giving students trouble—those items more students answer incorrectly.

With results such as these, should the instructor spend more time on review or move to the next unit? There is no rule or general guideline that tells us what average score or what most scores should be to decide when to move ahead in the class schedule. We need to set expectations for ourselves and our students. If the content in this unit is critical, and there are students that achieve less than 70% of the items on the test, we may want to provide opportunities for students to review or at least give some direction to the lower-performing students. If content is especially cumulative, where each unit builds on the previous one, keeping an eye on how students do following each exam will be essential to supporting their learning and maximizing course success.

### Individual Item Performance

With which topics do students continue to struggle? What errors do students make? What misconceptions do students hold? We can begin to gather diagnostic data by evaluating item performance and, more importantly, distractor analysis.

By more closely reviewing the items that posed more challenges to students, those that were more difficult, with lower *p*-values (at least those items with *p*-values of .70 or lower, with 70% answering correctly or less), we can see which options were most commonly selected. Distractor analysis tells us what specific errors and misconceptions students are selecting. We can tally the distractors selected for the more difficult items. Examining the frequency for which options were selected tells us a lot about how to proceed with instruction and address commonly held misconceptions or errors in problem solving.

This is accomplished most easily by using the measurement services that might be available at your campus. Otherwise, it can also be done in a number of software programs that allow you to enter the response selected by each student for each item, then simply requesting the frequency of responses for each item.

The following example includes the responses to four items from 50 students. Each item had four options (A thru D). For each item, we can evaluate the difficulty based on the frequency correct (the correct-option frequency is underlined and bolded). We can make the following statements for each question:

Q1. This is the easiest item (46/50 correct). Each option was selected, but by only 1 or 2 students each. This question is not of concern.

Q2. This item is more difficult, with only half answering it correctly (25/50). Distractor A is not functioning (did not attract any responses), whereas option D is very attractive (18/50 selected it)— indicating that this is a strongly held misconception (if the distractors are based on misconceptions).

Q3. This item is also relatively difficult (35/50 correct). Options C and D appear to be important misconceptions.

Q4. This item is the most difficult (20/50 correct), but it also might be miskeyed—since option D is the most frequently selected. It is important to see if the students who selected D also tended to score well on the overall test (which would give this item a negative item–total correlation or negative discrimination value). Otherwise, there is something about option D that is more attractive than option A—which requires us to look closely at option D.

*Table 7.1* Example Distractor Frequencies for 4 Items and 50 Students

| Question # and correct option | A Count | B Count | C Count | D Count |
|---|---|---|---|---|
| Q1—B | 1 | **46** | 2 | 1 |
| Q2—C | 0 | 7 | **25** | 18 |
| Q3—B | 2 | **35** | 7 | 6 |
| Q4—A | **20** | 3 | 4 | 23 |

Consider an earlier example item:

The best way to improve content-related validity evidence for a test is to increase the

A.   sample of students taking the test.
B.   number of items on the test.
C.   amount of time to complete the test.

If students selected options A or C at a high rate, this would indicate that students still consider these to be potentially correct. Option A typically improves the stability of all sample statistics, but it is not related to content (increasing the number of test takers doesn't affect content coverage). Option C generally leads to better measurement, alleviating the stress on students who need time to consider each item thoroughly—but again, it doesn't affect the content coverage. The instructor needs to

- reemphasize that content coverage is mostly affected by the number of items on the test and
- discuss the role of sample size and testing time and their effects on student test performance.

The depth and quality of the information regarding student KSAs and student misconceptions and errors can be enhanced through quality item and test development. All of the work we do based on the earlier chapters is only worth the effort if we take advantage of the information that results from our items and tests.

By reviewing the quality of our tests, we contribute to the cycle of continuous improvement of our own assessment practice and strengthen teaching and learning in our courses.

## Applications

1.   Calculate item difficulty statistics for the items in a course test. What do the results tell you about the items themselves? Were any items more difficult than expected? Use low difficulties to identify content that may need to be clarified.
2.   If sample size supports it, calculate item discrimination statistics for the items in a course test. What items differentiate best among high- and low-scoring students? What items differentiate the worst? Use low discriminations to identify items that may need to be revised.
3.   Examine distractor frequencies for each MC item in your test. Did any distractors receive little or no attention? Consider how these distractors

could be modified to better capture common student errors or misconceptions.

4.  Summarize how testing can be used in your classroom to inform your instruction and improve student engagement and learning. In your summary, consider how you report and provide feedback on test results to students and how this information is integrated into teaching and learning after the test is given.

# References

Brennan, R.L. (2011). Generalizability theory and classical test theory. *Applied Measurement in Education, 24,* 1–21.

Cronbach, L.J. (1951). Coefficient alpha and the internal structure of tests. *Psychometrika, 16*(3), 297–334.

Mehrens, W. A., and Lehmann, I. J. (1991). *Measurement and evaluation in education and psychology* (4th ed.). Orlando, FL: Harcourt Brace Jovanovich.

McManus, S. (2008). *Attributes of effective formative assessment.* Washington, DC: Council of Chief State School Officers. Retrieved at www.ccsso.org

VanLeeuwen, D.M. (1997). Assessing reliability of measurements with generalizability theory: An application to inter-rater reliability. *Journal of Agricultural Education, 38*(3), 36–42. Retrieved at http://citeseerx.ist.psu.edu/viewdoc/summary?doi=10.1.1.574.1427

# Index